A CREEK WARRIOR FOR THE CONFEDERACY

The Civilization of the American Indian Series

A Creek Warrior for the Confederacy

The Autobiography of Chief G. W. Grayson

Edited and with an Introduction by
W. David Baird

University of Oklahoma Press
Norman and London

Written or edited by W. David Baird

Peter Pitchlynn: Chief of the Choctaws (Norman, 1972; 1986)
The Osage People (Phoenix, Ariz., 1972)
The Choctaw People (Phoenix, Ariz., 1974)
The Chickasaw People (Phoenix, Ariz., 1975)
A Dictionary of the Osage Language, by Francis La Flesche (Phoenix, Ariz., 1975)
The Quapaw People (Phoenix, Ariz., 1975)
Years of Discontent: Doctor Frank L. James in Arkansas, 1877–1878 (Memphis, Tenn., 1977)
Medical Education in Arkansas, 1879–1978 (Memphis, Tenn., 1979)
The Quapaw Indians: A History of the Downstream People (Norman, 1980)
A Creek Warrior for the Confederacy: The Autobiography of Chief G. W. Grayson (Norman, 1988)

LIBRARY OF CONGRESS
Library of Congress Cataloging-in-Publication Data

Grayson, G. W. (George Washington), 1843–1920.
    A Creek warrior for the Confederacy: the autobiography of Chief G. W. Grayson / edited with an introduction by W. David Baird.
    p. cm.—(The Civilization of the American Indian series; v. 189)
    Bibliography: p.
    Includes index.
    ISBN 0-8061-2103-3 (cloth)
    ISBN 0-8061-2322-2 (paper)
    1. Grayson, G. W. (George Washington), 1843–1920. 2. Creek Indians—Biography. 3. Creek Indians—History. 4. United States—History—Civil War, 1861–1865—Personal narratives, Confederate. 5. United States—History—Civil War, 1861–1865—Participation, Indian. 6. Indians of North America—Oklahoma—History. I. Baird, W. David. II. Title. III. Series.
E99.C9G7 1988   87-27617
973'.0497—dc19   CIP

The paper in this book meets the guidelines for permanence and durability of the Committee on Production Guidelines for Book Longevity of the Council on Library Resources.

2   3   4   5   6   7   8   9   10   11   12   13   14

For
Eloise Grayson Smock
and
Edward Everett Dale,
who preserved the autobiography,
and
LeRoy H. Fischer,
who appreciated its significance.

Contents

Illustrations

Maps

Preface

THE LATE ROSALIE GILKEY DALE, the widow of historian
Edward Everett Dale, first called my attention to the autobiography of George Washington Grayson. Among the papers of
her distinguished husband was a typewritten version of the autobiography. Dr. Dale first saw the original manuscript in 1934
and with the active encourgagement of the late Eloise G.
Smock, Grayson's daughter, sought to prepare it for publication. Among other things, he arranged the text into chapters
and, to balance the sections and to respond to family considerations, deleted some passages. Unfortunately, the onset of
the depression and World War II made publication impossible.

Unaware of Dr. Dale's earlier interest, my esteemed friend
and colleague at Oklahoma State University, Professor LeRoy
Fischer, also hoped to publish the autobiography. In his research of the Civil War in Indian Territory, he had in the 1960s
encountered a handwritten text of the manuscript in the Western History Collections at the University of Oklahoma, which
at Dr. Dale's suggestion Mrs. Smock had previously placed
there on permanent loan. Fischer was especially attracted to
the author's accounts of Confederate military action in what is
now eastern Oklahoma and made long-range plans to publish
those particular sections. As happened to Dr. Dale, other duties and circumstances prevented him from consummating his
publishing plans.

I have benefited immeasurably from the pioneering labors of both Dale and Fischer. More than anything else, their interest in the autobiography confirmed my view that it was an exceedingly important document and worthy of publication. In preparing this volume, I began by comparing Dale's typescript with Fischer's copy of the original manuscript. Immediately I noticed differences between the two; the typescript, for example, contained virtually no misspellings and occasionally a sentence that elaborated a particular detail. I attributed these variations to that fact that Dale had edited the errors out of, and some detail into, the text. For that reason I ignored his rendition and worked with the original manuscript preserved in the Western History Collections.

By all measurements, the autobiography of George Washington Grayson is a remarkable document. For one thing, other extended eyewitness accounts of Civil War action in Indian Territory have yet to be discovered. Of course, there were reports of field commanders concerning particular engagements, and participants did write letters describing army life and action. And a fair number of these reports and letters have survived and have been published. But so far as we know, this detailed narrative of multiple campaigns by a single participant is unique. Grayson's manuscript is an eyewitness account of the most significant engagements in Indian Territory after 1862, viewed from the perspective of a Creek Indian warrior in the service of the Confederate States of America. Given the focus of the narrative, nothing comparable exists in the literature of the Civil War.

As a historical document, the autobiography is also unique for the sustained, inside glimpse it gives of the corporate life of the Creek Indians. There is a wealth of other documentary material relative to the history of the tribe, but most of it is time-bound and merely gives snapshots of particular events or persons, while in Grayson's account a single participant over a span of a half century observes and comments upon the political and social factionalism that bedeviled the tribe both before and after the Civil War. Few Indians, much less Creek leaders, had the literary skills or the foresight to leave such a record.

The autobiography is particularly unusual in that it reveals much about the attitudes of Creek mixed-bloods, or métis, toward a full-blood majority that held firmly to traditional cultural values. For various reasons the métis constituted an elite subgroup among the Creeks that exercised an influence well in excess of their number. Few if any ever thought to record their personal views of the full-blood majority whom they sought to lead if not dominate. This autobiography provides such a rare record.

Grayson's history of himself is an intensely personal document. He probably never intended that anyone should read it but members of his family. Moreover, it was written toward the end of a long career and relied upon what he thought was a failing memory. Actually his ability to recall the past was not as inadequate as he believed, for most that he recollected can be substantiated as accurate from contemporary sources. That he did not intend it for the general public is to the reader's advantage. He writes more freely and more candidly. But not writing for publication means that Grayson creates special problems for an editor.

The biggest editorial vexation relates to writing style. In the 197 pages of handwritten manuscript Grayson provided few paragraphs and absolutely no breaks for chapters. Not unexpectedly, he also adopted a prose style that is fairly common among turn-of-the-century writers; that is, he frequently linked one independent clause after another with conjunctions and dropped in commas in a way that mystifies modern readers. Some sentences, German-like, go on for an entire page.

Spelling and composition errors constitute another vexation. Classically educated, Grayson did not hesitate to use unique and colorful words. In the text, these words were not always accurately spelled. Moreover, he adopted spellings for other words that were acceptable when he wrote but seem strange and inaccurate today. At other times he unintentionally dropped a letter from a word as well as a word from an entire sentence. Interlineations often obscured rather than clarified a passage; almost all created grammatical problems.

Grayson's admitted reluctance to use dates furnishes still another impediment. Indeed, throughout his manuscript he used only three dates: those of his birth, his enrollment in college, and his marriage. The sequence in which he discussed events provides a vague chronology to the years of his youth and military escapades, but the passing of his adult decades were left without markers. It is difficult, therefore, to determine cause-and-effect relationships, to ascertain the relative significance of particular events, or to compare parallel developments (the public official with the private man, for example). The lack of mileposts suggests a corresponding difficulty: Grayson mentioned people, places, and events without identifying explanations. He assumed that his readers would know about whom he was talking, and, of course, the members of his family did know.

A final difficulty emanates from the genealogical passages. In an attempt to establish bloodlines and family relationships, Grayson included long sections about his ancestors and relatives. To the modern reader who is not a part of his extended family circle these seem extraneous and repetitive. Almost always they follow themes unrelated to Grayson's career, members of his immediate family, or Creek tribal history.

How does an editor address these problems in preparing an edition of the autobiography for publication? Regarding the text as a rough draft composed in an archaic style, I have chosen in presenting it, first, to be faithful to the *intent* of the text and, second, to retain as much as possible of the manuscript in an uncompromised form. Working from those premises, I separated multiple paragraphs out of what was essentially one long paragraph. In this process the text was left unchanged: no topic or transitional sentences were added. Using the schema, as well as the titles, suggested earlier by Dr. Dale, these paragraphs were then divided into ten chapters of approximately equal length.

Where the sentence structure permitted it, I also divided single long sentences into two or more shorter sentences. Frequently this was accomplished by silently substituting a period for a comma at the end of an independent clause, deleting the conjunction, and then capitalizing the first word of the following independent clause. In other places sentences were divided by dropping the subordinating word of a dependent clause and adding an appropriate noun as subject. In these cases an ellipsis and brackets were inserted to mark the deletion and addition. Even though it might have been possible to do so, not all extended sentences were divided. Some were retained merely to demonstrate Grayson's unique style of composition.

With regard to spelling errors, I originally intended to deal with them more conservatively, marking each with *sic* or adding corrections in brackets. Quite by accident I learned, however, that Grayson had prepared a second draft of his autobiography in which he apparently eliminated misspelled words and used few abbreviations. Although in the possession of the family and unavailable to me, that draft was the source of Dale's typescript and explained its variations from the manuscript draft with which I worked. Since misspellings, missing words, and dropped letters represented nothing more than the differences between first and second drafts and since *sic* and brackets were intrusive in the text, I elected to correct many of these errors silently. Inaccurate renderings of personal names, however, are corrected in the footnotes.

With the exception of misspellings, I have assumed that the original draft of the autobiography was the only draft. This assumption seemed appropriate for at least three reasons. First, I never saw the second draft; indeed, I deduced it existed after virtually all of my editorial work was completed. Second, judging from Dale's typescript of it, differences between the revised draft and Grayson's first draft never affected the substance of the text. Finally, an editor is obligated to work with the *original* document to the fullest extent possible. What follows, therefore, is Grayson's first draft of his autobiography, altered in spelling and grammatical construction only to accommodate the reader.

To provide a more precise chronological and historical framework for the text, I have supplied footnotes liberally. Insofar as was possible, every event, person, place, or circumstance mentioned by Grayson has been identified and placed in an appropriate context. The footnotes are written to explicate the text in such a way that a reader of the autobiography can appreciate the substance of Grayson's military and public career without having to consult a host of other sources. A concern for readability and chapter balance encouraged me to alter Grayson's genealogical passages. But this happened only five times, and all in the first chapter. Two of these deletions were extended quotations from published secondary sources, while one followed the lineages of distant cousins. Two others related personal details that had significance for family members only. These alterations are indicated by an ellipsis and a footnote at the points in the text where they occur.

The preparation of this volume for publication has been facilitated by the Grayson heirs, my colleagues, my students, and my family. As his grandmother, Eloise Smock, had encouraged Dr. Dale, so too has David G. Hansard, of Dover, Tennessee, graciously facilitated my production of a text that remains faithful to both the memory and the intent of his great-grandfather. At Oklahoma State University, Professor Joseph A. Stout, Jr., Head of the Department of History; Dean Smith Holt and Associate Dean Neil Hackett, of the College of Arts and Sciences; and Vice-President for Academic Affairs and Research James H. Boggs graciously supported my request for a sabbatical leave to complete this project and to begin others. History graduate students Phil Bevers and Mary Jane Warde did preliminary investigation on Grayson's career.

I have been fortunate to have the assistance of friends not associated with Oklahoma State University. My mentor and role model at the University of Oklahoma, Professor A. M. Gibson, on leave himself, graciously gave me the use of his home and library during my own sabbatical so that I could complete this particular endeavor. And Jack Haley, as curator of the Western History Collections at the University of Oklahoma, gave me access to the manuscript of the autobiography and to other Grayson materials under his stewardship. But my family rendered the greatest assistance. Jane, Angela, and

Tony accepted my absence of four months with patience and good humor, willingly assuming household and other responsibilities that normally are mine. The three are special, if not unique, and I thank them for their consideration and acknowledge their long-suffering.

Stillwater, Oklahoma W. DAVID BAIRD

A CREEK WARRIOR FOR THE CONFEDERACY

Introduction

GEORGE WASHINGTON GRAYSON'S autobiography has little meaning severed from the context of Creek national history. Indeed, the story of his life and that of his ancestors is the story of the tribe. To understand one it is necessary to understand the other. The Creek Indians were not natives of eastern Oklahoma, where today most live. At the time of initial European contact with them, they resided in what is now Alabama and Georgia and were organized into a myriad of decentralized political and social groups. With a preference for dwelling in communities, they lived together in as many as eighty different villages that were divided into "Upper" and "Lower" towns. The Upper Towns were in the Appalachian highlands on the north, while the Lower Towns were congregated on the flatlands and along the river bottoms on the south. A people noted for their generous hospitality and diplomatic skills, the Creeks generally welcomed into their midst individuals and groups of different ethnic origins and social customs, among them, of course, Europeans as well as Africans. These non-Indian aliens, both white and black, and the progeny of their marriages with Creek women—known today as the métis—did little at first to divert the Creeks from their preeminent commitment to traditional patterns of thought and activity.[1]

[1] The best general history of the Creek Indians is Angie Debo's *The Road to*

3

United States domination after the American Revolution produced dramatic changes among the Creeks. Assuming the unity, if not the equality, of all mankind, and intending to elevate the Indians to their own level of "civilization" within a generation, the federal government through its agent Benjamin Hawkins inaugurated a program to alter the economic and cultural customs of the tribe. In this endeavor many residents of the Lower Towns who were intermarried whites and métis became Hawkins's allies. Other members of the tribe, especially from the Upper Towns, responded to the "civilization" agenda and the whites' continual demands for land cessions first with passive resistance and finally with bloody conflicts. Although it was the result of outside influences and ended in the defeat of the dissenters, the so-called Red Stick War (1812–14) was just as much a Creek civil war, between "traditionalists" who opposed Hawkins's civilization program and "progressives" who supported it, as it was a contest between Indians and whites. Among Andrew Jackson's victorious troops were contingents of Creek warriors led by métis.

If the Red Stick War scarred the tribe, so too did the controversy surrounding its removal from Alabama and Georgia. Disappointed at the pace of acculturation, federal officials pressured the Creeks to remove from their ancestral domain to a new location in the west where advancement in "civilized" pursuits could occur at a more leisurely rate, and where they would not impede the agricultural development of their old homeland by white frontiersmen. The métis chief from the Lower Towns William McIntosh embraced this argument, and at Indian Springs early in 1825, McIntosh signed, in direct violation of a Creek law passed nearly two years before, an agreement by which the tribe consented to voluntary removal and relinquished most of its eastern lands in exchange for a

---

Disappearance: A History of the Creek Indians. A very useful short history is Donald E. Green's *The Creek People.* The experience in Indian Territory prior to the Civil War is covered in selected chapters in Grant Foreman's *Indian Removal* and *The Five Civilized Tribes.*

tract in Indian Territory. For this act McIntosh paid with his life, which was taken by the leadership of the non-métis majority associated principally with the Upper Towns.[2] The retribution meted out upon the métis chief did not forestall removal. It did cause the Indian Springs treaty to be set aside by the federal government, but in January, 1826, McIntosh's critics signed another treaty not radically dissimilar to the one to which they had so violently protested. Thereafter the McIntosh faction of the Lower Towns, fearing further reprisals, migrated west and settled on lands northwest of Fort Gibson between the Arkansas and Verdigris rivers. Within a decade the rest of the Creeks, pressured by the government and harassed by white frontiersmen, followed this advance party. Largely former Upper Town residents, they took up homes south and west of their kinsmen between the Canadian River and its North Fork. The settlement pattern of the Creeks in Indian Territory confirmed the political and cultural division existing within the tribe.

Significant attempts by the Creeks to reunite were aborted with the onset of the American Civil War. Economic considerations, especially slavery, caused the métis party of the Lower Towns and their supporters to identify with the southern states, while loyalty to old treaties encouraged adherents of the Upper Towns to align with the federal government and the northern states. Dividing the total population of 13,537 into almost equal parts, each of the two factions furnished troops for the contending armies.

After the Civil War the cleavage among the Creeks did not dissipate, although it changed somewhat. A new constitution in 1867 caused the tribe to divide into groups that either supported or opposed the governmental system instituted by the document. The old McIntosh party was joined by fellow tribesmen previously identified with the Upper Towns, and they embraced the new order, calling themselves "constitutionalists." Other Creeks, supported by freedmen (former black slaves),

[2] This era in Creek history is best assessed in Michael D. Green's *The Politics of Indian Removal: The Creek Government and Society in Crisis.*

objected and thought of themselves as "Loyalists." The so-called Sands Rebellion of 1871 and the Isparhecher Rebellion of 1881 (the "Green Peach War") emanated directly from what was virtually a métis versus non-métis division within the tribe.

George Washington Grayson's autobiography emerges naturally from and explicates much of the history of the Creeks during the nineteenth century. Both of his parents had European ancestors: his father was one-half white, while his mother was three-quarters. His paternal forebears lived among the Upper Creeks and identified with the conservative Red Sticks, while his maternal progenitors were Lower Creeks and supported the progressive McIntosh party. Born in 1843 in the vicinity of North Fork Town, near present-day Eufaula, Oklahoma, Grayson attended mission schools established among the Creeks by the Baptists and Methodists, and later studied at Arkansas College in Fayetteville, Arkansas. Like the majority of tribal métis, during the Civil War he campaigned with Creek units attached to the armies of the Confederate states and participated in virtually all of the significant engagements that took place in Indian Territory. These included the battle of Honey Springs, the capture of the *J. R. Williams,* the Flat Rock Creek episode, and the second battle of Cabin Creek. Like other Confederate Creeks, his family spent the later years of the Civil War as refugees along Red River.

In the postwar years Grayson associated with that faction of the Creeks that supported constitutional government. For ten years he served as treasurer of the tribe, and for twelve years he was a member of the House of Warriors, one of the two legislative bodies established by the 1867 constitution. In 1875 he considered making the race for principal chief, and in 1899 he was an unsuccessful candidate for the office of second chief.[3] As a métis and veteran of the Confederate Army, Grayson opposed the so-called Loyalist Creeks whom he tended to categorize as either non-métis or former Union soldiers.

[3] *The Vindicator,* July 3, 1875; and Election Returns of September 5, 1899, #29646, Election Records, Creek Nation Papers, Manuscript Division, Oklahoma Historical Society.

The latter were responsible for the Sands and Isparhecher rebellions, which he believed had threatened the independence of the tribe. Perpetuation of the Creeks as a sovereign government was his primary objective as a public official, especially on the many occasions he acted as a delegate to the federal government in Washington after the Civil War. The same goal induced him to serve as secretary after 1870 to the Okmulgee Council, an intertribal group envisioned by federal officials as a precursor to territorial government for the Indians.

Although very much a public man, Grayson never neglected his private life. His wife, Georgeanna Stidham, whom he married in 1869, he adored. The couple had nine children (Orlena, Mabel, Walter, Eloise, Wash, Tsianina, Anna, Annette, and Daisy) and enjoyed a marriage that spanned fifty-one years. Grayson's personal appearance and deportment were also important to him. Described as tall, dignified, handsome, and "of gentlemanly address," Grayson was likewise "fastidious in dress, intellectual in conversation, and polished in his manners."[4]

He had every reason to look and act successful, for his business ventures generally prospered. Building upon his experience as a clerk in different North Fork Town firms, he and his brother Sam organized Grayson Brothers and built it into a profitable concern. Among its many interests were a retail outlet, rent properties, a cotton gin, cattle ranches, and agricultural activities. After 1880, Grayson Brothers also controlled the *Indian Journal,* the national newspaper of the Creeks. In late 1891 the firm valued its property at $71,150, the bulk of which was invested in four thousand head of cattle ranging on lands west of Eufaula. Grayson had other partnerships in which he participated, usually business ventures involving G. W. Stidham or Joseph M. Perryman.[5]

[4]H. F. O'Beirne and E. S. O'Beirne, *The Indian Territory: Its Chiefs, Legislators, and Leading Men* 1:134.

[5]List of Property Belonging to G. W. and Sam Grayson, Dec. 23, 1891, #39350, Treasurer Records, and Pasture Leases, April 7, 1893 and Feb. 19, 1894, #34960 and #35002, Pasture Records, Creek Nation Papers, Manuscript Division, Oklahoma Historical Society; Annelle Sharp Lanford, "North Fork to Eufaula, 1836–1907" (M.A. thesis, University of Oklahoma, 1954), 95.

George Washington Grayson, chief of the Creeks, 1917–20, in about 1917. *Western History Collections, University of Oklahoma Library.*

After the allotment of Creek tribal lands at the turn of the twentieth century and the demise of tribal government in 1906, Grayson readjusted his personal priorities. Public affairs were pretty much beyond his control, his family was prospering, his business interests were successful, and he was in his sixties. It was a time for reflection—upon the worth of his career and upon the historical significance of his people. In 1908 he began to write the autobiography presented in this volume. Three years later, and perhaps while he was still writing his life's narrative, he met John R. Swanton, the renowned ethnologist of the American Bureau of Ethnology, who was launching a major study of the social organization and customs of the Creek Confederacy. Grayson became Swanton's major informant, recalling for him Creek traditions long since forgotten by younger tribespeople. Swanton even read the manuscript of the autobiography and shorter manuscripts by Grayson on Creek history.[6] Possibly the interaction with Swanton relative to customs no longer in use reinforced Grayson's conclusion that tribal history ended, for all intents and purposes, with the disappearance of tribal government. If that was the case, it explains why Grayson terminated his autobiography with an account of the allotment of Creek lands, an event that took place twenty years before he died.

Those last years, however, were not ones of total retirement from public affairs. On occasion he attended tribal councils, translated documents into and from the Creek vernacular, appeared before congressional committees, and responded to federal government inquiries. In 1905 he served in the Sequoyah Convention that wrote a constitution under which Indian Territory would have entered the union as an independent state. One of the five members to draft the preamble and the "Declaration of Rights and Powers of Government," he also sought unsuccessfully to have Eufaula designated as the capitol of the proposed state.[7] But by and large this and other efforts were, to use Grayson's phrase, "finishing up" work, attending to details associated with the disappearance of an independent Creek government. Ironically, it was in this capacity that Grayson was finally recognized for a life of service to his people. In 1917, upon the death of Moty Tiger, the last elected principal chief of the tribe, President Woodrow Wilson appointed the aged métis as chief of the Creeks.[8] He served in this capacity for more than two years, during which time his most symbolic act was finalizing the sale of the Creek Council

[6] John R. Swanton, "Social Organization and Social Usages of the Indians of the Creek Confederacy," *Forty-second Annual Report of the Bureau of American Ethnology*, 31.
[7] Amos D. Maxwell, *The Sequoyah Constitutional Convention*, 77 and 134.
[8] *Indian Journal*, Dec. 9, 1920, 1.

House in Okmulgee to the county government.[9] Tribal government had been "finished up." So too was George Washington Grayson. He died on December 2, 1920.

James Olney has written that autobiography is best understood as a metaphor of self, an attempt to mediate between the internal and external, between the writer's experiences and those of his readers, between the past and the present self, between oneself formed and oneself becoming.[10] Certainly Grayson's work is a metaphor of himself. Writing after 1908 when that to which he had devoted his life, which had explained his life, was no more, he sought to find meaning by putting the different elements of his life into relationship with one another. His ordering of events, his metaphor, provided the necessary connection that produced meaning, for him and for us.

And what is the meaning of the Grayson autobiography? Obviously it will be different for each reader, but certain dimensions of the meaning will be perceived by all. Surely Grayson wanted it understood that, unlike ancient Creeks, he traced his ancestry through the paternal line. Far from being embarrassed by it, Grayson was proud of his métis heritage. He was what he was because of it.

It is clear too that Grayson saw his Civil War experiences as particularly formative in his life. Despite comments to the contrary that may have reflected upon his métis status, the war enabled him to demonstrate his manhood by exceptional bravery under fire. Other Creeks failed (perhaps non-métis Creeks?), but he did not.

Grayson's autobiography also assesses his public service. He wanted it understood that self-interest was never one of his motives, although it did motivate colleagues. It was clear to him as well that he did not seek public office, but that office came to him because of his ability to provide leadership. It

[9]Note on envelope addressed to G. W. Grayson, Eufaula, Feb. 17, 1919, File VIII-40, Box G-23, Grayson Family Papers, Western History Collections, University of Oklahoma. The building was appraised for $100,000.

[10]James Olney, *Metaphors of Self, the meaning of autobiography* (Princeton: Princeton University Press, 1972), 18, 31, 35, and 36.

was important to Grayson too that his readers recognized that his service to the tribe required huge sacrifices of time, well in excess of anything for which he was ever compensated. Finally, it is evident that, as Grayson ordered the past in relationship to the present, he concluded, with reference to the Creek people, that they had traveled a "road to disappearance"—to use the title of Angie Debo's history of the Creeks. The factional struggles and constitutional controversies of the post–Civil War period had weakened them. The final denouement was allotment in severalty of the tribal domain and the termination of tribal government. It is no accident that Grayson ended his autobiography with those events. For the tribe and for himself, metaphorically, allotment and termination constituted the end of the road.

CHAPTER ONE

Early Forebears

ON SEVERAL OCCASIONS as my inclinations led me, I have while seated at our family meals related to the members of my family incidents of my past life, many of them the results of conditions and circumstances created by the late war between the states in which I played a small part. On one or two such occasions some members suggested that such narratives were very interesting to the living members of our family and would be even much more so when in after years I was no longer present to relate them, and that as a favor to future generations of our family I should by all means commit some of them to writing so they may be effectively preserved for the future entertainment of such as may care to read them. While promising to do this, I have been slow to enter upon the work.

To accomplish such a task with any fairly satisfactory approach to completeness, however, it seemed to me that the work should be given the form and character somewhat of an autobiography. Although foreseeing much arduous labor and drudgery involved in this method, I have decided to pursue this plan in the preparation of the work, leaving the question of my success or failure to be determined . . . by such of the members of our family as shall read it. I have no recollection of ever having read an autobiography written by anyone else, and hence have adopted no model by which to be guided in my effort, and supposing that it would probably be conceded that each such writer may justly be a law unto himself, I have proceeded to write in my own way, and as suits me best. I have so written especially because this effort is not for the public eye, but only for perusal by the members of our family, of whom I expect the widest charity in their estimates of my numerous short-comings which will appear in all parts of the work.

Having decided on the autobiographical form, it seemed to me to be a matter of the first importance to trace my genealogy as far back as I could with such helps as I was able to find and utilize, in order that members of our family who shall care to be so informed may have at least an approximately correct knowledge of their origins. With that object in view, I have exerted considerable labor and research on the subject of our old Scotch ancestry, some data of which as the reader will readily observe, approach perilously near the domain of the mythical.

An almost indispensable characteristic of any history, bio-graphical as well as otherwise, claiming authenticity is the item of date. But I have always been, and am yet woefully deficient in remembering dates; so where I have begun the work of actually writing about myself and incidents coming under my personal observation, it will be observed that the date when the things and occurrences mentioned & related took place is conspicuously absent. No attempt [has been made] to state any date when any incident mentioned oc-curred, and it is quite probable that there are instances where incidents in the narrative are given priority as to the time of happening which were in point of fact really of subsequent occurrence. The actual transpirations, however, with their re-lated facts, I believe to be faithfully and correctly recorded, as the most of them are yet quite vivid in my memory.

In this work I have undertaken the task of writing that which I purpose shall stand as my autobiography. But as preliminary to what shall be written as such, I deem it of importance . . . to trace my genealogy as far back as such available material at hand will permit, so as to impart . . . a correct knowledge of the people from whom I have descended. For be it understood that while there have been a number of persons bearing the name Grayson, of whose acts we cannot speak or conceive of

CREEK NATION
c. 1898

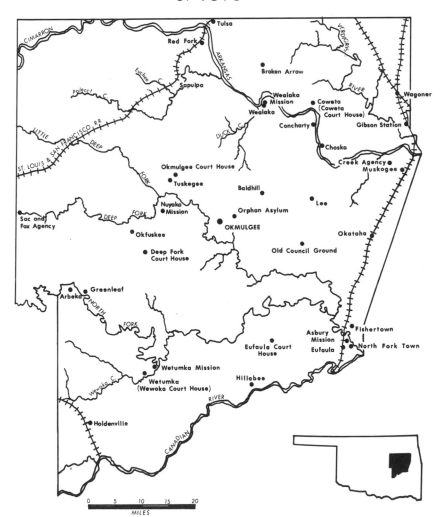

with any measure of approval or toleration, the original Scotsman of that name to whom we trace our origin was in all respects a worthy gentleman of whom his descendants may well be proud. In tracing my lineal descent from him, I find myself forced to treat extensively of him as well as of other personages of the related families following in the same line of consanguinity.

Beginning my work then in the manner indicated, it may be said that sometime away back in the dim and hazy past *Robert Grierson* left his native land of Scotland for the new world of America. On the subject of when or where he embarked, or whether or not he came in company with his brothers, or where he landed on these shores, we have no knowledge, as tradition and authentic history alike are both silent on these points as far as I have been able to ascertain. . . . For the present it is sufficient to know that he did land somewhere on the continent, for we find him in the year 1796 living in the Indian country, subsequently the state of Alabama, married to a Creek Indian woman of the name of Sin-o-gee of the well known Hillabee Town of the Creek nation, who bore for him many children.[1]

As were many others of the old Scotsmen who domiciled in the Creek nation at that time, he was distinctively a man of business.[2] By trade and good management, as will hereafter

[1] Hillabee was one of more than fifty "towns" that collectively composed the Creek Confederation in the 1790s. The various towns virtually were independent tribes, and many spoke different languages. They were only loosely associated politically in the two divisions known the as Upper and Lower Creek towns. The towns were also socially connected by a host of clans, as well as by moieties that organized the communities into Red (war) and White (peace) divisions. Located just north of the principal English trade route connecting Augusta, Georgia, with the Chickasaws, and some ten miles north of present-day Alexander City, Alabama, Hillabee was a Red town identified with the Upper Creeks. As such its residents, despite the presence of the Grierson family, were inclined to resist the innovations and perspectives of white society and to depend upon traditional leadership. See Swanton, "Social Organization and Social Usages of the Indians of the Creek Confederacy," 170–287.

[2] Families established by other Scotsmen, most of whom entered the Creek domain via the Chickasaw trade route out of Augusta, Georgia, included the McGillivrays, McIntoshes, McQueens, McHenrys, McGirths, McCalls, Barnards, and Kennards.

appear, he amassed a considerable fortune; much greater perhaps than did any other one person in that locality. And [he] was possessed of sufficient influence with the Indians to enable ˙ him when occasion required to be of at least some service in the interests of peace and good understanding when hostilities broke out between the Creeks and the Whites. His home was the hospitable resting-place for those representatives of the United States government who visited the Creeks on missions of peace or other public business, as well as to those dignitaries of the Creek nation whose duties called them to that part of the Creek country. As a corroborative of this statement may be quoted Mr. Pickett who in his History of the state of Alabama states that:

> Learning that McGillivray was then on a visit to Okfuskey on the Tallapoose river, Col. Willet determined to join him at that place. . . . At the house of Mr. Graison in the Hillabees, the secret agent had the good fortune to meet Col. McGillivray. The party accompanied by Col. McGillivray and his servant, took leave of the hospitable mansion of Graison.[3]

The above appears to be of about the date May 3, 1790. Under date of November 18, 1813, we are informed that:

> Through Robert Graison, an aged Scotchman, the Hillabees (a portion of whom fought Jackson at Tulladega) made offers of peace to which the general immediately and willingly accepted. At that very time and when Graison had hastened back with the favorable reply of Jackson, Genl. White surrounded the Hillabee town early in the morning and effected a complete surprise, killing sixty warriors and taking two hundred and fifty prisoners.

From the same author we find that in about the same year:

> The hostiles (the Creek Indians) destroyed the stock of the friendly Indians at the Hillabee towns, several of whom they

[3] Grayson's reference is to Andrew J. Pickett, *History of Alabama and Incidentally of Georgia and Mississippi from the Earliest Period*, 401. Alexander McGillivray, a métis from the Upper Towns, was the principal leader of the Creek Confederacy in the 1780s and 1790s. Col. Marinus Willett carried a confidential dispatch from President George Washington inviting him to come to New York City to sign a treaty of peace with the United States. A treaty was negotiated later in 1790. See Debo, *Road to Disappearance*, 48–52.

killed. They carried off seventy negroes belonging to Robert
Graison, and committed many other depredations.[4]

The author, George Cary Eaggleston, in his "Red Eagle and
the wars with the Creek Indians of Alabama," referring to the
above incident, says, "They sent Robert Grayson who had
lived among them for many years to Jackson's camp to sue for
peace," etc. etc.[5] In this instance the author writes the name
as spelled and written by those of us who now bear the name in
this country. How the name which originally was Grierson
came to be so changed I am not sure, but it is a conjecture of
mine that it came about through uneducated persons and Grierson's own negro slaves, it being almost natural for the unlettered to pronounce Grayson for Grierson. . . . In old family
papers I recall quite distinctly seeing the name written *Grierson,* instead of as now. If there was anything in a name, I
would move for a return to the original.

In further pursuance of information of this ancestral Grierson, it is perhaps proper at this time to state that while residing
some years ago with my family in the city of Washington,
D.C., in the official character of delegate of the Creek Nation
to the committees of Congress and the departments of the general government, I was approached by a gentleman who claimed
to be from the state of Alabama, the former home of the
Creeks. This gentleman informed me that while searching
among certain old musty archives in quest of data for use in

[4]Grayson refers here to Pickett, *History of Alabama,* 556 and 520. The conflict mentioned in the quotations was associated with the so-called Red Stick War
(1813–14), a reaction of conservative Creeks, generally from the Upper Towns,
to the "civilization" program or innovations encouraged by the United States and
embraced by other Creeks principally from the Lower Towns. The needless destruction of the Hillabee town by American-led troops was in reprisal for the Red
Stick–perpetrated slaughter at Fort Mims, and it preceded by five months the
decisive battle of Horseshoe Bend that ended the war. Andrew Jackson commanded the American troops and their Indian allies. See Frank Lawrence Owsley, Jr., *Struggle for the Gulf Borderlands: The Creek War and the Battle of New
Orleans, 1812–1813,* 66–67 and chap. 7. For Jackson's view of the war see
Robert V. Remini, *Andrew Jackson and the Course of American Empire, 1767–
1821,* chaps. 13–14.

[5]See George Cary Eggleston, *Red Eagle and the Wars with the Creek Indians
of Alabama,* a work that is limited in its historical value.

writing a proposed history of his native state . . . , he had discovered . . . the journals of Benjamin Hawkins, who as an official representative of the government of the United States traveled extensively among the Creeks in Alabama in early days . . . , in which appeared very interesting mention of Robert Grierson. . . . This information very naturally appealed to my interest as well as my curiosity, but being quite absorbed by the duties of my mission, I did not at that time obtain a copy of the MSS. . . . After considerable desultory correspondence with my informant, I succeeded in obtaining a transcript of so much of the Hawkins manuscript journal as related to Grierson from the librarian of the Georgia State Library, for which I gladly enough paid $5.00.[6]

To anyone interested in the old Grayson (Grierson) stock of people in the Creek nation, this transcript is of absorbing interest and is here reproduced from the peculiar copy sent me (peculiar in some of its orthography as will be seen). . . .

Friday 9th Dec. 1796
Mr. Hay informed me that I was within 12 miles of the Hillabeas, a town on a creek of that name, that in this town or its neighborhood live Robert Grierson, a native of Scotland, who very intelligent, had lived many years in the nation as a trader & had an Indian family, that he spoke the language & had large possessions negroes, cattle & horses. I determined to take this route. Mrs. Hay accompanied me. I sat out at 12, traveled 1 mile & X creek N.W 15/ running to the left, the lands fine for cultivation, continued on uneven lands Xing several small creeks and over a small mountain in 9 miles, arrive at the Hillabeas, 20 yards wide, Xing it & over waving lands 4 miles to the house of Mr. Grierson. Mr. Grierson was at home and rec. me with a social hospitalitable frankness. He had his family around him ginning & picking cotton. I was much pleased to see it. He had made a considerable quantity and is preparing it to send to Tennassee where

---

[6] A resident of North Carolina who had served five terms in the Continental Congress and its successors, Benjamin Hawkins was appointed U.S. agent for the Creeks in 1796 and served until his death in 1816. He was the principal advocate of the government's "civilization" program. For a biography that draws upon the collection referenced by Grayson, see Florette Henri's *Benjamin Hawkins and the Southern Indians.*

he expects 34 cents the lb.

Saturday 10th. December 1796
     I took a view of Mr. Grierson's farm, he had planted the last season two acres of cotton in drills 4 feet asunder. There is 30 acres in the farms, the product, corn, cotton, rice, peas, beans, squashes, pumpkins, watermelons. Peaches grow wild, but he had but a few trees & not any other fruit trees.

Sunday 11, dec. 1796.
     I have had much conversation in relation to Indian affairs with Mr. Grierson, he speaks the language well, & is intelligent. he was during the revolution ever attached to the armies of the U.S. & made some curtions [excursions?] in aid of them. he is now much attached to this country & means to spend his days here with Indian family & companions, he justly estimates his situation & can & will contribute his aid in furthering the views of the government. The family of Robert Grierson are his wife Sinoegee of the family Spanalgee; their children Sandy, Sarah, Walter, David, Liza & William. Sarah is married to Stephen Hawkins, their children Pinkay & Sam. 40 negroes, 300 cattle, 30 horses. They have in the range a place called a stamp, where the horses have salt every spring & here they gather of themselves, at that season. The cattle at that season come to the creek for moss, the bottom being covered with it. And at this season all the state holders make a gathering. . . .[7]

     From the data adduced in the foregoing sketch it is quite certain that the original Grierson, or Grayson as now called, was a gentleman who in his day, in point of character, material wealth and moral stature, stood far above a majority of the men of the country of his adoption. In that he was sometimes chosen intermediary in the interest of peace by the Creeks when hostilities threatened between them and the whites . . .

[7]Subsequent lengthy passages included by Grayson from Hawkins's journal dated Dec. 12 and 14, 1796, and another long quotation from vol. 3, pt. 1, of the *Collections of the Georgia Historical Society* have been deleted by the editor. They may be found in a reprint of the 1848 edition of the journal published as Benjamin Hawkins, *A Sketch of the Creek Country*, 44. Primarily genealogical, these passages refer to the three brothers of Robert Grierson—James, Thomas, and William—who lived in the vicinity of Augusta, Georgia, and to Grierson's cultivation of cotton and his manufacture of cloth.

clearly manifests the esteem and confidence in which he was held by the people of his adoption. In that he by example and precept led the way toward the cultivation of habits of industry and thrift among the Indians . . . is striking evidence of his sturdy virtues [and] usefulness as a desirable citizen, a practical business man whose sterling worth was instantly observed and appreciated by all intelligent men who came in touch with him. He was not one of that restless low type of white men too often in evidence among the Indians, whose puny morals chafing under the restraints and responsibilities of civilized life impel them to sneak away into the Indian country where they may hunt, trap, fish and eke out an existence little removed from the life of the savage, and where their life and character are a blight to the Indians and not a blessing. [Grierson] on the contrary Col. Hawkins tells us was indued with the true spirit of commerce and was a trader belonging to that class of useful pioneers ever found in the van of progress, boldly and openly blazing the way for advancing civilization and empire. . . .

Col. Hawkins could not but observe the success with which [Grierson] exercised his parental authority over his Indian family and took occasion to call attention to it in his journal. It is unfortunate, however, that the facilities for even the commonest school education were so meagre in those days that he appears to have been unable to favor his children with some degree of a common school education. I know of only two of them, Liza or Lizzie and William, who could read and write a little.

I have now recorded here about all the authentic data I have been able to collect relating to Robert Grierson [and] the origin of the family of Graysons in the Creek nation, which are all so much in his favor that no descendant need ever be ashamed to trace his relationship to him. Pleasant Porter who was an intelligent and well read person has always said to me that he understood that Grierson had been a *Sir,* and therefore numbered among the governing lords of the mother country.[8] But my researches have failed to verify his statement. . . .[9]

[8]Pleasant Porter, the son of a white man and a woman of the Perryman family,

One of the children of Robert Grierson of Alabama, Katy, and the one in whom we are most interested at present is not named among those mentioned by Col. Hawkins in his journal. This fact is perhaps to be accounted for by the supposition that she was not yet born when the colonel was stopping at Grierson's home. William, whom he mentions last in the list [of children], was probably at the time of his visit the youngest, and as I have always understood that Katy was younger than he, she, it is very probable, was not yet born. . . .[10]

It is proper now to introduce another personage who supplies a short link in the chain of the story to be told. That is no other than one *In-tak-fahp-ky*. This man was a full blood Creek Indian of the Hillabee town. . . . We understand that in his day he was reckoned somewhat an Indian magician or conjuror. It is related of him that by means of the superior powers he possessed as a conjuror, he would sometimes amuse himself by the perpetration of innocent practical jokes at the expense of his friends and intimates.[11] [The] wife of In-tak-fahp-ky was a white woman named *Mary Benson,* who when a small girl had been captured by a war party of Creeks long prior to the Red Stick war. She grew to womanhood among the Creeks, was adopted a member of the tribe and married the subject of this sketch. She evidently was from

---

was born Sept. 26, 1840, in present-day Wagoner County, Oklahoma. He served the Creeks as an educator, a military leader, a delegate to Washington, and a chief, the latter between 1899 and 1907. He died Sept. 3, 1907. Porter and Grayson were long-time friends and colleagues and over the years espoused similar views on the political issues that confronted the Creeks. See John Bartlett Meserve, "Chief Pleasant Porter," *Chronicles of Oklahoma* 9 (Sept., 1931): 318–34. Grayson abbreviated Porter's first name as "Pleas" throughout his manuscript.

[9] Deleted here is Grayson's brief introduction to a verbatim rendering of a lengthy biographical sketch of Sir Robert Grierson (1655?–1733), the laird of Lag, Scotland, whom Grayson believed might have been the father or grandfather of Robert Grierson of Alabama. See *Dictionary of National Biography* (reprint, London: Oxford University Press, 1949–50), 8: 664–65.

[10] At the request of Grayson's heirs, brief passages relevant principally to the family have been excised at this point. This has necessitated subsequent deletion of an adjective or two at different places in the text, particularly through n. 15 in this chapter. An ellipsis marks the location of all of the alterations.

[11] A long passage from the original manuscript describing one of In-tak-fahp-ky's practical jokes on his wife has been deleted.

the state of Georgia, for after she was the mother of several children, an uncle from that state visited her, and being pleased with her Indian children took two of her boys, Dick and Jack, with him back to his home. When they returned to their home in the tribe some time afterward, [the boys] were able to speak the English and were about the first of the youth of the surrounding country who wore trousers, coats and so forth instead of buckskin leggings and such other characteristic primitive apparel as were worn by the people of the nation in those days.

This couple had born to them, Un-ah-yoh-ky, or Nah-yoh-ky, whose other name given him when he attained his majority, as is the custom of the Creeks, was E-mah-thla-hut-ky; second, Nannie; third, Nancy; fourth, Johnie, or Tsah-nu-tsee (Little John); fifth, Somully; sixth, Dick; and seventh, Jack. Johnie or Tsah-nu-tsee's name given him at his majority was Tul-wa Tus-tun-ug-gee (Town warrior). . . .[12]

[The assignment of names] was the custom and practice of the old Indians of that day, and indeed is the practice even now in some localities in the Creek Nation. At the annual festivities, called by the Indians Poos-ke-tah and by the English speaking people *Busks,* the old men of the town and male rela-

[12] Omitted here is an extended account by Grayson of the polygamous family of Emah-thla-hut-ky, who was also known as Hog Meat. A son-in-law of Emah-thla-hut-ky, Daniel Grant Wilson, was a trading partner of Jesse Chisholm, and Wilson's daughter married John McIntosh, the son of Col. Chilly McIntosh. The family histories of Emah-thla-hut-ky's other children are a part of the deleted passage, as are those of his brothers, Dick and Jack Benson. Because of later allusions in his autobiography, Grayson's references to Jack Benson's family are significant: "Jack Benson had several children, but I never knew any but Mary and David. Mary was married to Timothy Barnett, and with him lived near the crossing of the public road leading from old North Fork town west, across the well known stream Wewoka, where Barnett conducted a small trading establishment, the buildings of which are constructed of huge oak logs. During the Civil War, Barnett was promoted to the colonelcy of the 2nd Creek regiment in the Confederate service, in which my own company (K) was a component. Barnett was during almost all of his mature life prominent more or less in the public affairs of the Creek Nation. He was rather of a domineering nature which sometimes led him into trouble, and which caused him to assassinate an Indian of the neighborhood whose death was avenged by a mob of Indians who surrounded his house and shot him to death." Later in this discourse Grayson also indicates that he was writing his autobiography on Aug. 6, 1908.

tives of the young candidate agree among themselves that he is of that age that entitles him to the name that shall relegate him from the ranks of boyhood to that of manhood, and proceed to select a name for him. He is notified of the name he is to take, and at a time when all are gathered and seated in their proper places in the square, he will be by one old man called by the name agreed on and by which he is hereafter to be known. The call is slow and long drawn out, and when repeated four . . . times, [the] young man goes over to the presence of that particular dignitary doing the calling, when he will be offered a small piece of tobacco which he receives and waving his hand over towards the naming official, exclaims "Yoh! yoh!" which ends the ceremony. This name the young men are generally very proud of, since by it they are *boys* no longer, but *men*, ever hereafter to be so recognized and respected by their acquaintances.[13]

After this custom and manner Johnie Benson [or Tul-wa Tus-tun-ug-gee] was christened with his manhood name as stated. Of his earlier youth we have no information; but know that sometime during his early manhood he was prevailed upon by the powerful oratory of the Indian promoters of war to join the ranks of the hostile Creeks, sometimes designated as the "Red Sticks," who arose up in arms against the United States government. And true to his martial name of *warrior*, [he] fought to very desperation under the leadership of Munah-we against the United States forces under general Andrew Jackson. Notably at the battle of the *Horse Shoe Bend* where the Red Sticks had made a determined stand, he was wounded nine . . . times, which in later life proved the source of everrecurring pain and illness, some attacks lasting many days in duration. These attacks were caused, as it was said, by the fact that the bullets were never extracted by the Indian doctors who treated his wounds.[14]

---

[13] For an extended discussion of the busk festival, also known as the Green Corn Ceremony, see Charles Hudson, *The Southeastern Indians*, 365–75, and Swanton, "Religious Beliefs and Medical Practices of the Creek Indians," *Forty-second Annual Report of the Bureau of American Ethnology*, 546.

[14] See n. 4 above and Debo, *Road to Disappearance*, 80–81. Mun-ah-we was

In the foregoing mentioned engagement [Tul-wa Tus-tun-ug-gee] was completedly disabled by his many wounds. When the day was spent and darkness came on and the Creeks recognizing the fact that they could not continue the contest longer were retiring under the cover of night, but for his brother E-mah-thla-hut-ky and other comrades, he would have been left upon the field to the mercy of the enemy who would come upon the grounds the next morning. This brother with the assistance of others took him upon his back, and in company with their retiring comrades, he was born to a place of safety in the woods miles away where the Indian medicine men doctored him and after many weeks, restored him to fairly good health. He was of medium build, rather below the medium in stature, a little inclined to be bow legged, coal black hair inclined a little to curl, with all the ways and manner of a full blood Creek Indian.

Returning now to the story of Katy, the . . . daughter of Robert Grierson the Scotsman, we find that . . . she was living quietly somewhere, we presume with her father's family. [In due time] . . . she married Johnie, the brave and honored warrior—son of In-tak-fahp-ky and the white Georgia woman, Mary Benson. This young warrior, Tul-wa Tus-tun-ug-gee, member of a race ever jealous and proud of its exploits and prowess in war, and who himself never wavered in the presence of a hostile foe and on occason proved himself a fighter to the death, succumbed to the wiles and attacks of Cupid and was taken captive by Katy Grayson. . . .

[B]eing the daughter of Robert Grierson, by far the wealthiest and most influential character in the surrounding country and [with] Johnie or Tul-wa Tus-tun-ug-gee being only the son of an obscure father and of a mother who was only an adopted captive of the pale faces, Katy Grayson would seem to have married below her rightful station. . . . Be that as it may, certain it is that they lived together to be very old people, to

---

the second chief of the Upper Creek Okfuskee town and had been influenced by Tecumseh in his resistance to the federal government's civilization program. In 1825 he was one of the executioners of William McIntosh, the signer of the Indian Springs treaty that stipulated the removal of the tribe from Alabama.

become wealthy in slaves and much other property, and to rear a large and highly respected family of sons and daughters without a single jar in the family relations of "Uncle Johnie" and "Aunt Katy" as they were affectionately called by their many acquaintances. . . . [T]heir first . . . child . . . was . . . named James.[15] Afterwards came Charity, Robert, Lizzie, Tility, Levi (Book), Louisa (Tookah), Thomas, Caroline and Adaline, which last two were twins. We know of no others.

The full blood Creek Indians never add as a surname that of the father to the name given his children nor is the name of the mother ever so used. The child, however, invariably takes its clan from the mother. If she is of the bear, deer, beaver or panther clan, that is the clan to which the child belongs. So Tul-wa Tus-tun-ug-gee being son of an old full blood Indian father who had no name that could be transmitted as a surname to his children, he likewise could have none to transmit to his offspring. His brothers Dick and Jack by the circumstances of their residence for a time in the state of Georgia with their uncle had taken the name of that relative and come to be known as, and surnamed, Benson. But Tul-wa Tus-tun-ug-gee and E-mah-thla-hut-ky did not take that or any other English name. . . . The Graysons being by far the most wealthy and influential family in the Hillabee town, when Tul-wa Tus-tun-ug-gee an obscure Indian of no wealth or prestige married into the family, it seemed by common consent on all sides to be the logical and proper thing to apply to all members of this marriage the name of Grayson as a surname, which was done and kept up to the present time.[16]

So James the first born of Tul-wa Tus-tun-ug-gee and Katy Grayson, and his brothers and sisters who followed, were not in strict accordance with the custom and usage of the families of civilized communities of this country, strictly speaking,

[15] See n. 10 above.
[16] Since a child was a member of his mother's clan, Tul-wa Tus-tun-ug-gee was essentially clanless, as his mother, Mary Benson, was a white woman. For his children to assume the surname along with the clan identification of his wife, Katy Grayson, would have been in keeping with the matrilineal tradition of the Creeks. For the significance of the clan in tribal society see Michael D. Green, *The Politics of Indian Removal: Creek Government and Society in Crisis,* 4–7.

Graysons; nor would any of their offspring of whom I am one,
be. But since common consent and usage seem to successfully
legitimatize many things, and, there is very little that can
make for good or evil in a mere name anyhow, we have borne
the name to this day trying to maintain for it a proper respect-
ability by the fostering of education and the interests of correct
living among ourselves and the rising generation of the family.

When I first came to know Tul-wa Tus-tun-ug-gee and Katy
Grayson they lived in the Choctaw Nation nearly two and a
half miles south of the South Canadian river, and about the
same distance east of the confluence of the Gain's creek and
said Canadian river.[17] When they moved from the state of Alabama west with the other Creeks, they settled in the valley of
the Poteau, a stream in the western part of the state of Arkansas, whence they moved settling at the place above described.[18]
They owned many negroes, hundreds of heads of cattle, horses
and ponies, sheep, hogs and poultry, but only a small farm of
some 30 or 40 acres, and were a happy family, supplied with
all the comforts of well-to-do families in the surrounding states
and to a degree far ahead of the people in their immediate
neighborhood.

We have now traced the genealogy leading from Robert
Grierson up to the birth of his grandson James, the first born
of his daughter Katy and Tul-wa Tus-tun-ug-gee, who was my
father. I have heard it said that he was a rather diminutive
baby, and some there were who doubted his having vitality sufficient to sustain him through the period of his babyhood. . . .
When taken to his grandfather Grierson, he is reported to have
caught up with his thumb and fingers his skin on some part of

[17]Gaines Creek, once identified as the South Fork of the Canadian, presently
constitutes the southern arm of Eufaula Reservoir. The site described is in northeastern Pittsburg County, Oklahoma, and is across the reservoir (east) from the
community of Canadian.

[18]The Grayson family removed from Alabama before 1832, perhaps as early
as 1826. At least one of Katy Grayson's paternal uncles, Thomas, seems also to
have settled in western Arkansas just south of Fort Smith. The Poteau River,
however, flows entirely in Oklahoma. See Danield F. Littlefield, *Africans and
Creeks, from the Colonial Period to the Civil War*, 112–13.

his body, and observing it to be loose and yielding, declared
reassuringly that "baby" was all right, as he had an abundance
of skin which nature had supplied and intended should fill out
and supply all necessary growth and strength.

Having reached my immediate paternal ancestor, it now becomes necessary for me to write what I know of my mother.[19]
Owing so much to her, it would afford me unstinted pleasure
to write fully of her genealogy, but it is my misfortune to know
scarcely anything about it. In the early days of the Creeks,
among other prominent and noted families of the nation were
the Kennards and the Harrods. As to the orthography employed here in writing these names I am not entirely clear.
While the latter name was for a long time pronounced by ev-
eryone in this country as above written, in later years it came
to be pronounced and written Herrod. But as our people emi-
grated to this country from the south where the former name
Harrod, I find, was common and as that was for a long time
the only pronunciation heard here, I am satisfied that it is the
correct orthography and pronunciation.

These Kennard and Harrod families were of the Coweta
town which was one of the towns belonging to that division of
the Creeks known as Lower Creeks. They were of Indian and
white blood, and while generally prominent in the governmental affairs of the nation, none of them was ever chief of
the nation until sometime in about the year 1859, when Moty
Kennard, a man of extraordinary physical stature, being considerably over six feet in height, was elected to that office, and
as such served until and after the breaking out of the great

---

[19]The extent to which G. W. Grayson had embraced non-Indian traditions at
the time he wrote his autobiography is reflected by his emphasis here upon his
paternal ancestors. Significantly, his prominence in the political life of the tribe
was due in large part to his mother's clan, town, and family (Kennard and Harrod) ties. Because of this matrilineal connection with the Panther clan and the
Coweta town of the Lower Creeks, Grayson lived among the Lower Creeks and
represented the Coweta town in the national council although he resided at North
Fork and later Eufaula. As acculturated as he was, Grayson owed his status among
the Creeks to very traditional social customs. See Swanton, "Social Organization
and Social Usages of the Indians of the Creek Confederacy," 67 and 228.

Civil War in the states.[20] It was generally remarked that he possessed no fitness for the office. He had one son, Noble, who appeared to be utterly worthless, and after the Civil War died somewhere in the Choctaw Nation near the Canadian river east of Eufaula. The father, Moty, died somewhere in, I think, the eastern part of the Choctaw nation where he with many of the Creeks took refuge from the advancing lines of the federal forces, while still Chief of the Creeks.

The Harrod family was very considerable in point of numbers and were some or all of them in some way related to the Kennards. I knew only six of the members of this family namely, Hotache and Sychar, brothers; Leah and Maria, their sisters; and Rosanah and Goliath. These last two were brother and sister, but not of the other four. I understand that the four first mentioned had at least one other sister named Per-cin-ta, who was married to John Wynne by name, but commonly called Jack. It appears that they were married and living together either in Alabama or Georgia before the Creeks moved west of the Mississippi river. They had one child whom as a baby they brought with them to this country naming her Jennie. When they reached this country, they were among the first Creeks to settle and build a home on the banks of the little branch of the river on the site afterwards settled up by others and named the town of North Fork.[21] Here this couple had two

---

[20] Nearly seven feet tall and a Baptist deacon, Moty Kennard became the first elected chief of the Lower Creeks in 1859 following tribal adoption of a written constitution. By ancient custom he was deemed the principal chief in that the chief of the Upper Creeks deferred to the leadership of the Lower Towns. Kennard was also a prime supporter of the treaty in 1861 that aligned the tribe with the Confederacy. See Debo, *Road to Disappearance,* 124 and 145; Carolyn Thomas Foreman, "North Fork Town," *Chronicles of Oklahoma* 29 (Spring, 1951): 101; and *Annual Report of the Commissioner of Indian Affairs, 1859,* 178–80.

[21] Located some two miles east of present-day Eufaula, Oklahoma, North Fork Town was the focus of some activity in the early 1830s, then became a commercial center of significance after the Creek emigration of 1836. It was at the intersection of two thoroughfares: the north-south Texas road and an east-west road from Fort Smith to the mouth of Little River that after 1849 became a branch of the California Trail. Foreman, "North Fork Town," 80, and Lanford, "North Fork to Eufaula, 1836–1907," chap. 1.

Jennie Wynne Grayson, mother of G. W. Grayson, circa 1870s. *Courtesy of David Hansard.*

other children, daughters, Rebecca and Parthenia or as she was popularly called "Feenie."

The name Wynne, of the spelling of which I am not sure, I am informed is of Welsh origin, and it has been said that in the vicinity of Columbus, Georgia, there were not many years since many people living of that name. In the records of transactions of the Creeks with representatives of the United States I have seen the name Wynne appearing somewhere as signatory to a convention with the Indians, from which it would seem the inference that he at some time took active interest in the public affairs of the Creeks, is justified.

This man Wynne and his wife Per-cin-ta Harrod died, leaving their three little daughters Jennie, Beckie and Feenie and some property including one negro woman to the tender care of their next of kin, which property these relatives proceeded to squander and dissipate in short order. They were thus penniless at their years of majority and experiencing a hard and difficult struggle in life when James Grayson met and married Jennie Wynne. They journeyed back to the home of the Graysons in the Poteau valley in the state of Arkansas, where they lived for sometime at the home of James Grayson's mother, Katy Grayson.

When James Grayson's father Tul-wa Tus-tun-ug-gee was fighting the battles of the "Red Sticks" years before, the Coweta Indians were friendly to the whites and aided Jackson in the signal defeat he visited on the hostiles at the sanguinary affair of the Horse Shoe Bend where Tul-wa Tus-tun-ug-gee was so seriously shot up. Because of this former friendship and aid rendered the whites, there was always an unfriendly feeling toward the Cowetas lurking in the hearts of those who had been "Red Stick" warriors.

Jennie Wynne, although received and treated kindly by the Graysons, could not but observe that the old prejudices engendered by the wars of years ago cropped out at times to her disadvantage, she being a member of the Coweta town. These, however, never caused any breach of friendliness existing between her and the family, and she and James Grayson after living contentedly for some time finally moved away to build a home for themselves. They moved to a point in the dense woods of Possum Creek, some three and a half or four miles west of the present town of Eufaula, and probably six from the then town of North Fork. Here they lived in a very humble log cabin, but how long we do not know, when their first born made his appearance in the baby person of the present autobiographer, in reaching whom we have deemed it needful to write so many tedious pages about so many other people.

All the writing done on the subject up to now, stated in a nut shell, is simply this: a certain Scotsman named Robert Grierson, by a full blood Creek Indian woman named Sinogee, had a daughter Katy, who married Tul-wa Tus-tun-ug-gee, bearing for him their first born, a son, whom they named James, who married a poor orphan girl of the Coweta town named Jennie Wynne, and to whom was born a *man child*, whom they named Washington, but who in after years while attending school took on the additional name George, and is now known as G. W. Grayson the present relator.

CHAPTER TWO

An Indian Boyhood

MY PARENTS HAD no school education, such as is fostered and encouraged nowadays. Neither of them having ever attended a school a day in their lives, they were entirely unable to read or write, so they never recorded the fact of my birth or [thought] it of sufficient moment to call in some friend to record the day of that, to me, very important event. Luckily . . . , however, my aunt Tility, precisely one month previously, had borne a child whom she named Valentine N. whose father, a white man named John McAnally, being sufficiently educated to write, recorded the day of his son's birth as being the 13th day of April 1843. That this birth occurred exactly one month to a day prior to my own advent appeared to be well known and unquestioned by all the friends and relatives. It being quite universally the custom among those unlettered people to reckon only *four weeks as one month,* by making the computation with a proper observance of these facts, I reached as a just and fair approximation the conclusion that I was born on or about May 12th 1843, and which is the date I claim as my natal day.

I do not think we lived any considerable length of time in the home on Possum Creek before we abandoned it, removing and settling a short distance, perhaps about one and a half miles west of the home of my grandparents Katy Grayson and Tul-wa Tus-tun-ug-gee on the south side of the Canadian river, near by whom and with whom their other sons and daughters made their homes and were living. Here my father improved

another humble home as well as a small farm where we lived
I know not how long, but at least until I was of sufficient dis-
cretion to be sent on simple errands over to Grandmother's.

My father's youngest brother, a young man named Thomas,
was often at our cabin. I am told [he] enjoyed much innocent
amusement at what might have been my expense had I not
shared in the fun as much as he did. It is proper to state here
that my hair was a very dark red and so continued until I was
twenty years old, when it changed to dark brown. [Thomas]
would deck my head out in a turban made out of an old cotton
handkerchief; bind old pieces of cloths and rags about my legs
in imitation of the dressed and smoked buckskin leggings so
universally worn by the full blood Creeks of that day; tie a
little bundle on my back in imitation of the little supply of
bedding and subsistence the old Indian hunters all carried on
their backs when going to the woods on a hunting expedition
of several days; provide me with a rod of wood for a gun,
causing me to appear for all the world like an old fashioned
Indian hunter in miniature, then direct me to go and show myself to Mother and inform her that her son through aid of Uncle
Thomas was now equipped and ready to repair to the wild
woods where, barring ill luck, he would kill a big deer and
bring [it] to her. This it is said greatly amused him and others,
as well as myself.

Whether my brother Samuel was born here or not I do not
know. From this home in the Choctaw Nation, we moved back
across the river in the Creek Nation, not to the Possum Creek
home however, but some three or four miles south therefrom
just at the foot of the timbered mountains west of the M. K.
and T. railway, about two miles south of Eufaula. My present
recollection is that my father traded for the place which had
been owned by a full blood Creek Indian named Tum-me
Yoholar. This was only another exceedingly primitive little
log cabin home, with the spaces between the logs composing
the house chinked and daubed with red clay. It had the character, however, of being in the fashion of the times, as all
other houses of the country were similarly built and finished. We lived in this humble abode it seems to me now many

years, but may not have been, when Father enlarged our home by building an additional log cabin in the north end of the yard. While we lived here, Grandmother deeded to Father a negro slave named Wilson, whose labor lightened considerably the work and toil necessary in meeting the expenses and support of his growing family which were becoming onerous to Father.

At this home I have my first recollection of seeing and playing with my brothers Sam and Pilot.[1] Here the dominating and triumphant forest in all its pristine exuberance and grandeur abutted almost against our door yard. In these sylvan domains whose august quietude was undisturbed by any sound of human activities save an occasional shot fired from the gun of a solitary Indian hunter at wild game in the deep and distant woods, we lived squarely face to face with nature and nature's denizens, the true and unerring teachers of erring man. The garrulity of the omnipresent crow; the chorus of enchanting music from the myriad songsters which in the Spring time made inimitable opera of every tree of these vast forests; the clatter of the beaks of the yellow hammer and woodpecker against the dry limbs of the deadened trees on the little farm; the familiar bark of the frisky and inconstant little gray squirrel in the great protecting oaks; the reflected beauty of the green trees, the blooming dogwood and redbud with their sheen of snowy white and inspiring crimson, the mossy banks and blue skies, from the limpid waters of the creeks and branches by which we sported, all conspired to instill within our simple natures that love of home, that acquaintance with the true, the beautiful and the good, that affection for the land of our birth that will never give place to any power short of death.

---

[1] Sam Grayson was born in 1849, attended Asbury Manual Labor School, and after the Civil War enrolled for three terms in Cane Hill College in northwestern Arkansas. He married Kate Ross, a Cherokee, in Jan., 1879, and became a successful merchant. He died in 1924. Pilot Grayson, according to cemetery records, was born in 1850. After the Civil War he attended Cane Hill College, Howard College in Alabama, and LeGrange College in Mississippi. A teacher and merchant, Pilot married a daughter of and, after the daughter's death and that of her father, the widow of Baptist missionary H. F. Buckner. See O'Beirne and O'Beirne, *Indian Territory* 1:250–51, 261–63.

Sam Grayson, brother of G. W. Grayson, circa 1892. *Oklahoma Historical Society.*

While my parents had no school education whatever, they each had a very high appreciation of the advantages following the possession of it, and were unalterably determined that their children should not like themselves, grow up without some sort of school education. My father, I recall to mind, desired that his children should become educated so that they would not be forced to labor out in the hot sunshine, as he had all his life been forced to do, in order to realize a livelihood. I recollect also that it was his ambition and hope that with a school education, i.e. "to read and write" as he called it, some of his offspring might attain to positions of honor and trust in the public affairs of the nation. How his hopes worked out will be seen as our narrative progresses.

My father never identified himself with any of the churches, but seemed to be rather somewhat opposed to them. Mother was exactly the opposite, being a very pious and consistent member of the Baptist church, to unite with which she had to travel some four miles carrying me, a very small boy, with her. She was baptized in what was and is yet called Baptizing Creek, some two miles west of the present town of Eufaula. Her principal motive I recall for desiring that her children should become educated was that they might thereby be able to read to her and for themselves the Holy Bible, about which she had heard much but knew little, and learn of the salvation therein taught.[2]

While we lived here Grandmother conceived the idea of establishing a residence near North Fork town so provided that

[2]Following removal from Alabama, and especially among the Upper Towns, the Creeks reacted negatively to Christian influences, for a time banning missionaries from their borders and persecuting converts. The attitude of Grayson's father undoubtedly reflected this movement. Throughout this period, however, native Baptist preachers remained active in the area of North Fork, influencing tribespeople such as Grayson's mother and other members of her family. In 1848 this work resulted in a religious revival that touched such prominent Lower Town leaders as Chilly McIntosh and Moty Kennard, causing one Baptist divine to write from North Fork in 1853 that, "The Lord has, without doubt, given this vineyard to the Baptists." Simultaneously, official persecution of Christianity throughout the Creek Nation ended. See Debo, *Road to Disappearance*, 116–20; Foreman, "North Fork Town," 82–84, 94; and *Report of the Commissioner of Indian Affairs, 1848*, 527.

her children, two girls, Adaline and Caroline, and such other
children of the Grayson family as chose to, could occupy it as
a temporary home and attend a school that was conducted at
the town. Accordingly she had some cabins built in the dense
woods which is now Ella Tolleson's farm, which served as a
residence, and wherein was installed one of her negro slaves
who kept house and did the cooking. Father lodged me at this
place, and with the girls and possibly others, I attended as a
day scholar a school in the west edge of the town, first I think
to a Mr. Hay, then to Mr. Adkins.[3]

It seems now to me that I could not have been over six or
seven years old for I know that all that I learned in these two
schools was simply as to what a school is and what teachers
seem to expect of their pupils. As for anything taught out of
the books, it appears to me that I learned little other than my
letters. . . . A certain full blood Indian boy and I were conspicuously dull, and the teacher would display on a stand made
for the purpose a large volume, a primer with immense black
letters and pictures, telling us to study from our seats the les-
son on the open page of the book as displayed on the stand
before us.

All the kindly encouragement given me by my teacher concerning the, to me, deeply hidden things printed in the lessons
were just that much kindly effort wasted. I recall one certain
page of that never-to-be-forgotten volume on which was displayed the immense picture of an ox grazing in a pasture.
Turning to this page and picture, the teacher favored me and
my dull Indian classmate with a short lecture on oxen in general and on this one in particular. He informed us that the
legend in large black print underneath the cut read—"The ox
eats grass. The ox gets fat." He instructed us to read this as

[3] A day school that functioned during a 22-week session, taught by Baptist
missionary Americus L. Hay, opened in North Fork in January, 1848, with 30
pupils. At about the same time a second school, operated by the Methodists,
accepted local students as well. Its teacher may have been a Mr. Adkins. Foreman, "North Fork Town," 82–84, 94; *Report of the Commissioners of Indian
Affairs, 1848*, 528; and James William Moffitt, "A History of Early Baptist Missions Among the Five Civilized Tribes" (Ph.D. diss., University of Oklahoma,
1946), pp. 86 and 89.

he had, as well as some more which followed which he assured us was just as simple as the first, when he would hear us recite later.

Our turn arrived after a while and he took us in charge. By the exertion of extraordinary effort we advised him the *ox ate grass and got fat.* But when we were required to read further on, I with my comrade in learning failed completely and simply were not in it. As I was able to speak English, my failure was inexcusable, while in the mind of our teacher there was some allowance to be made for my classmate's failure, who spoke only Indian.

To impress therefore upon my young mind and the rest of the school the importance of close and searching application to study, and the shame and confusion that is a sure concomitant of its neglect, this dispenser of knowledge decided for mine and the school's benefit to make an example of me. To that end [he] shaped a sheet of paper into what I afterwards learned is known as a *dunce's cap,* which he fitted on my empty head, ordering me to stand out on the floor of the school room where the whole school could see me. This was done, when the scholars all roared with laughter, and instead of crying with shame and confusion as most children do in like circumstances, I too laughed inordinately at my own predicament, and was rather proud of being the cause of so much amusement to my schoolmates. This I think decided our teacher that I was a degenerate, for he at once uncapped and sent me to my seat.

My schooling at these two institutions amounted to little more than getting me away from home and out among other people, and teaching me the alphabet and perhaps a little spelling. To that extent of course some good was accomplished. The Hay school house was built of stakes driven in the ground and weather boarded and roofed with clapboards rived from the trees in the forest, and stood near where many years later Indian missionary H. F. Buckner lived.[4] The other school

---

[4] A noted Baptist missionary, Henry Friedland Buckner came to the Creek Nation in 1843, settling at North Fork Town a decade later. During the Civil War he took refuge in Texas, but he returned in 1870 to continue his work until his

house was of logs and stood a few yards west of the site occupied after the close of the war by Judge Stidham's mercantile establishment on the west edge of what then was North Fork town.[5] What became of these pioneer institutions of learning, or how long they were operated as such, or when or how I came to leave them I have now no recollection.

About a half a mile east of our humble home already described lived Thla-thlo Hajo, an old well-to-do Indian who I think was of the Eufaula town, whom we familiarly called Old Fish. He had several log cabins the more pretentious of which were built of split and hewed logs, two being joined together under one roof with a gallery or corridor between, in which the family made their home. This residence was directly on the east side of the public wagon road leading through the country from Fort Gibson through North Fork on the north, to the state of Texas on the south.[6] Over this road passed an occasional wagon loaded with a family of movers and their effects,

death in 1882. His house in North Fork was constructed in the mid-1870s and paid for by contributions from Baptist friends in the States. The site mentioned here is now beneath Lake Eufaula, but the graves on it, including Buckner's, have been removed to Greenwood Cemetery in Eufaula. E. C. Routh, "Henry Friedland Buckner," *Chronicles of Oklahoma* 14 (Dec., 1936): 456–66, and Moffitt, "A History of Early Baptist Missions," p. 87.

[5]Born in 1817 in Alabama of Scotch-Irish and Creek Indian parentage, George W. Stidham settled at Choska south of Coweta following removal and became a successful cotton and wheat grower utilizing the labor of numerous slaves. He also operated a store at the old Creek Agency until 1861. During the Civil War he enlisted in the Second Regiment of Creek Mounted Volunteers, C.S.A., commanded by Col. Chilly McIntosh. After the war he opened a mercantile business, first at North Fork and then at Eufaula, and operated farms in Texas. Stidham served as chief judge of the Creek Supreme Court, helped to draft the Okmulgee constitution in the 1870s, and served on at least 15 tribal delegations to Washington. He also became G. W. Grayson's father-in-law. After a long life of service to the Creeks, he died in 1891. L. M. S. Wilson, "Reminiscenses of Jim Tomm," *Chronicles of Oklahoma* 44 (Autumn, 1966): 290–306, and O'Beirne and O'Beirne, *Indian Territory* 1:185–87.

[6]The thoroughfare mentioned here was the great Texas Road. Collecting streams of traffic out of Missouri and Kansas, it crossed the Cherokee country and entered the Creek Nation from the northeast at the Three Forks of the Arkansas, Verdigris, and Grand rivers, and continued southward until it reached the Canadian River near present-day Eufaula. Its route paralleled present U.S. Highway 69 and the tracks of the Missouri, Kansas and Texas Railroad. In 1845 during one six-week period 1,000 wagons passed over it into Texas. For a historical sketch of this major trail see Grant Foreman, *Down the Texas Road*.

G. W. Stidham, Creek tribal delegate and businessman, and father-in-law and business partner of G. W. Grayson. This photograph was taken about 1866. *Smithsonian Institution, National Anthropological Archives.*

as well as travelers on horseback, the principal mode of travel in the country at that time, and which had the effect of imparting more of the appearance of life than did the environments of our home. Fish having moved away from the place, my father decided to possess it, and did trade for this home on the public road some time after it was vacated.[7]

[7] Although title to land among the Creeks was held in common rather than individually, a tribesperson had use of it so long as he or she possessed and/or occupied it. Improvements to the land, however, were personal property and could be sold to another party.

This emergence from our completely secluded home at the base of the mountains was to me who had attended the North Fork schools and seen something other than the forests, the streams and birds, a very welcomed change. Not satisfied with the site of buildings, Father razed and removed them to the west side of the road where we lived until forced by the exigencies of the Civil War to remove and take refuge in the Chickasaw Nation. By this time my brother Samuel had become a fairly good sized boy,

We did not remain very long in this new and more desirable home when Father, true to his determination that his children should be possessed of some degree of school education, began considering and with Mother discussing the question of placing us in the Creek national school some four or five miles north from our home known as the Asbury Manual Labor School.[8] It being decided in the affirmative, Father went with us to the school, where we were received and turned loose with the little Indian pupils of the institution, almost every one of whom spoke the Indian language, and only a few using the English in conversation. Father stipulated with the management that at the expiration of every three weeks we should be permitted to visit our home, and it was not long before we were more than anxious for the expiration of the time so we could go home and get "something good to eat," for it is true that the fare at the school was at times simply execrable.

Among the first things we learned here was the speaking

[8] Asbury Manual Labor School was first established in 1822 near Fort Mitchell on the Alabama side of the Chattahoochee River by the South Carolina Methodist Conference. It closed in 1829, but following removal of the Creeks to Indian Territory, and after the anti-Christian movement had run its course, it was reopened in 1850. Funded in large part by the tribe but administered by the Missionary Board of the Methodist Episcopal Church South, and superintended by T. B. Ruble, the school during Grayson's time there occupied a three-story brick building of 21 rooms, measuring 110 feet by 34 feet. The school closed during the Civil War, reopened in 1868 only to burn the following year, opened again to burn again in 1881, was repaired and then destroyed permanently by fire in 1888. The site of the school is presently beneath the waters of Lake Eufaula. See Foreman, "North Fork Town," 85, 103, and 108; Debo, *Road to Disappearance,* 85, 97, and 352; and *Report of the Commissioner of Indian Affairs, 1841,* 524–26.

with tolerable proficiency the Creek, which we did speak at our home. Our father always exercised a deal of sternness in the management and control of his children, and to us, his most trivial dictum in any case was law, the disobedience of which was not to be so much as thought of. Some of the children by representing to their parents the undesirable character of the food served, prevailed upon them to take them away to their homes. Others without permission ran away from the school, and their fond parents condoned their acts of disobedience and permitted them to remain for many weeks at their homes where their valuable time was wasted. We knew, however, that our parents would refuse to permit any such representations or acts to influence them to interfere with the continuity of our attendance at school, and that if attempted we would most likely receive heroic treatment with the rod. We bravely and uncomplainingly bore our ills to the last.

I got awfully tired of this school and often wished for the time when I would be a man and not have to attend. But everlasting thanks to our good parents, they continued us at this school for something like three years; and at a time too when we could have rendered needed help to Father in conducting the work about the farm.[9]

We had many different teachers during these years. They did not seem to succeed in advancing us much until toward the last when the school was provided with a Yankee school teacher originally from the state of Vermont, named W. C. Munson. He with his wife and two daughters, one of the latter being named Elvira M. and the other Eva F., took charge of the work in the school room. Being a professional teacher and in good practice, we learned more through his teachings than all the teachers who preceded him. This man seemed to love the work of school teaching, as well as the pupils under him, and was

[9]Grayson apparently entered Asbury about 1856 at the age of 13. In 1858 enrollment at the school exceeded 80, with the age of the students ranging from 8 to 16. In addition to academic studies, male students helped to care for a 75-acre farm and to grind meal with a steel mill. Both male and female students received instruction in vocal and instrumental music. *Report of the Commissioner of Indian Affairs, 1858*, 147–48.

always conscientiously desirous of benefiting those committed
to his charge. . . .[10]

Miss Eva, the youngest of [Munson's] family, conceived a
marked liking—almost infatuation—for me. This I only suspected, as we were not allowed to meet and talk with the girls
of the school. When, however, the usual three weeks expired
and I and brother were preparing to pay our accustomed visit
home, someone informed her that I was going home. Believ-
ing that I was going to leave the school for good, she broke
down and cried, causing something of a scene among the
school girls to my infinite embarrassment and confusion. [Eva]
was only pacified when told that we would be back in our
places within three days.

This [behavior] seemed remarkably strange in a young girl
to me as to the other pupils of the school, as we knew that an
Indian maiden would calmly bear to have an arm cut off rather
than betray such emotions in public because of her attachment
to a person of the opposite sex. This showing in a girl was a
kind of weakness altogether remarkable and unexpected to our
simple natures. This young lady survived, as I understand, all
of her nearest relatives, married a gentleman who had served
as captain in the Federal army during the Civil War named
George Clinton Smith and is living in Springfield, Illinois, a
worker of statewide note in the Temperance cause.

As may well be expected, our unbroken continuance in
school, so persistently maintained by our ever-to-be praised
parents, resulted in Sam and I being numbered among the most
advanced of the pupils of the Asbury M. L. School. Sam was
always apt and quick to learn, but it was never so with this
writer. The ever-present temperament that won for me the
dunce cap when only a tot of a school boy in the log school
house stayed with me during my later years, when I struggled
through long division to the unraveling of the mysteries of the
binomial theorem, the digging out of Latin roots and kindred
work, ever marking me as only a slow, plodding learner at

[10]Munson first joined the faculty of the school in the fall of 1857.

Tullahassee Mission, Creek Tribal School, northwest of Muskogee. This school was comparable to Asbury Manual Labor School, which G. W. Grayson attended near Eufaula. *Western History Collections, University of Oklahoma Library.*

best. By close and unremitting work alone could I keep up with my classes.

I have written that I was very tired of this school, but that is hardly the correct expression. I was tired of attending *any* school and not Asbury in particular, and longed to be free and out in the world where I would not have to attend school and pore over text books. No, I have always a warm nook in my affections for old Asbury, for after all, have not some—indeed many—of my happiest days been spent within her walls and on her campus? And indeed did I not here receive in a larger measure my preparation for the battle of life which I have subsequently engaged in, and in which I flatter myself that I have been fairly successful? If I may say it, is the declaration any the less true, when I declare that the foundation laid here through the persistent encouragement of my good parents and the honest efforts of my kind teachers enabled me to outstrip as the world estimates it quite all the boys who with me were schoolmates then? [D]uring all these years . . . I was a rather slim boy with exceedingly red hair. As the Indians are never red haired or blondes, I was an exception, being also quite white in complexion, and always regretted being as I was—white and red headed. I never got into many fights and know of one or two only in which I was victorious. In running, jumping and wrestling I held my own quite fairly well with those of my size, and as I now recall, I had no mate with whom I was particularly chummie, but engaged in our simple amusements with all alike.

I must have infringed on many of the rules of [Asbury] for I recall vividly the fact of receiving many whippings from the various teachers and the superintendent of the school. I remember one teacher, Roberts, who administered to me a severe flogging once, as I thought without sufficient cause, with whom I hoped for many years afterward that I might meet and square accounts. Time, however, evens up many inequalities and differences, and as this occurred fifty years ago, I some how feel now as if time has gotten in its work and I would not call him to account even if I were to meet him.

CHAPTER THREE

To School in the States

THE CREEK GOVERNMENT had some years previously adopted an educational policy, a feature of which was the sending off to colleges and schools in the surrounding states where the advantages of obtaining an English education were better, one or two of the most advanced and promising pupils in the boarding schools of the nation. Under the operation of this plan several young men had up to this time been so fortunate to be selected and sent to what was called Arkansas College, a small and weak school located then in Fayetteville in Washington County and presided over by Rev. Robert Graham of the Christian Church, sometimes called Campbellites.[1] It was a

[1] Known for two years as Fayetteville Male Academy, Arkansas College was chartered in Dec., 1852, and was the state's first degree-granting institution. During its nearly nine years of operation the school enrolled as many as 200 students in sessions that began in September and continued into June. In February and March, 1854, four Creek students—Eli Danley, David Yargee, Richard Carr, and Lyman Moore—entered the institution, the tribe paying $225 in tuition per student. The first president of Arkansas College, Robert Graham, was a native of Liverpool, England, a graduate of Bethany College in West Virginia, and had settled in northwestern Arkansas in 1847. The so-called Campbellites were part of an early nineteenth-century American religious reform movement energized by Thomas and Alexander Campbell as well as Barton W. Stone. Their spiritual heirs today include members of the Christian Church, the Churches of Christ, and congregations of the Disciples of Christ. See *Report of the Commissioner of Indian Affairs, 1855,* 139–41; *History of Benton, Washington, Carroll, Madison, Crawford, Franklin and Sebastian Counties, Arkansas* (hereinafter, Goodspeed, *History*), 275; Pat Donat, "Arkansas College: The Beginning," *Flashback,* Aug., 1977, 5.

signal honor to be one of those selected for this place, but as
is unfortunately so often the case these places were dealt out
to the relatives, sons, etc., of persons of influence. Although
I was perhaps in theory entitled to a place, I could not believe
[I might be selected to attend the school] as my parents were
not influential.

[As] the tuition, board and clothing . . . [were] paid for by
the nation, [an appointment] was . . . greatly to be desired.
Ben Marshall, Jr. son of the treasurer of the Creek Nation,
David Yargee son of a highly prominent family, and Eli J. Danley of the old aristocratic and governing town of Tuckabatche,
and Lewis Miller of another prominent family of the Cowetas
I think, [as well as] Billy McIntosh son of D. N. McIntosh a
very influential man for many years, and Eli Jacobs, all from
the vicinity of the Arkansas river [received appointments].[2]
These young men, excepting Miller, were not selected because
of their special fitness or worth, as I verily believe, but because of the prominence in the affairs of the nation of their
parents and guardians. They had what is nowadays called the
necessary "pull"—influential family, influential friends. I have
been told that Mr. Miller was a most estimable and worthy
young man who bade fair to be useful to his people but died
early lamented by all who knew him; I never met him. The
other young men so far as their fitness for usefulness to their
country and society was concerned, they were almost failures.

Sometime in the year 1859 as I now believe, the selection
of another to be favored with an opportunity to study at Arkansas College was agitated. It was rumored that the selection
would probably fall on some one in our school. After this ru-

[2] Benjamin Marshall was a Coweta headman who signed the infamous removal
Treaty of Indian Springs in 1825, but unlike his friend and fellow signer Chief
William McIntosh, he escaped death at the hand of Creek dissidents. He was
reported to have employed a hundred slaves on his Verdigris River plantation.
David Yargee was the grandson of Big Warrior, the venerable speaker of the
Upper Towns prior to removal. Eli J. Danley had previously attended Asbury
Manual Labor Institute. Daniel N. McIntosh was a son of William referred to
above and the half brother of Chilly. He later commanded the First Creek Regi-
ment, C.S.A. See Green, *Politics of Indian Removal*, 181; Debo, *Road to Disappearance*, 110, 155; Littlefield, *Africans and Creeks*, 138, 155n; and Foreman,
"North Fork Town," 96.

mor had gone the rounds for some considerable time, my parents were informed that my proficiency in school seemed to entitle me to that honor, and were asked if they would consent for me to go and remain so far away from home for the period of a year should the selection fall on me. My good parents took the subject under advisement for several days. I was anxious to go and risk my chances in this school "in the states" as we all called it, but the question trembled in the balance as it were. To send their first born who had never been farther from home than five or six miles, to a town a hundred or more miles away among strangers where he would remain continuously for a whole school year, was something difficult for my good father and mother to yield their consent to do.[3]

I was asked if I desired to go. I readily assented, being only too glad to have the question left to my decision. I remember well it being said by one of my parents—I do not recall which—"He having this excellent opportunity, and being himself willing to make the venture, should we because of our affection for him withhold our consent and he grow to manhood without the education which with our consent he might have obtained in Fayetteville, he will always lay at our door the blame for his lack of a better education." This, and the fact that we could now read the Bible readily as Mother had so fondly wished and the probable ambition wrought in our parents' minds for even greater advancement for their children, by our success at Asbury, decided them to let me go come what may.

This decision being made known to the school authorities my appointment was announced in due time. I have thought that this appointment perhaps never came to me solely because of my record as a learner and advancement in school, which as already intimated was very good. [Doubtless it came] in part because of the relationship of Mother to Moty Kennard who was at this time chief of the lower Creeks.[4]

After this decision, my father at once began preparations to place me in this Arkansas college, the journey to which had to

[3] Doubtless the fact that Grayson was only 16 at the time of his nomination to attend Arkansas College gave his parents pause as well.
[4] See Chap. 1, n. 20.

be made by horse back. The cousin Valentine N. McAnally, elsewhere mentioned as being exactly a month older than I, was engaged to go along with Father and me. So saddling up our horses one day, we three left our humble home for Fayetteville. I think we rode some forty miles the first day, stopping over night at old William Grayson's. . . .[5] From here next morning we continued our journey into the Cherokee nation to a very nice appearing neighborhood late in the evening, known then as now as Park Hill. The homes of the Murrells, the Rosses and others being in all respects in keeping with the homes of the rich in the states, with walls and paling yard fences all beautifully painted, were by far the more beautiful I had ever seen either at North Fork town or Asbury school. [They] lent me some idea of the great and grand things I had always suspected as existent in the outer world, and which I longed to see.[6]

We rode up to the fence of the yard where lived John Ross the chief of the Cherokees. [We] asked for lodgings over night, which was accorded us with such hearty good will and cordiality as made us feel quite at home. Entering the house we were ushered through corridors into rooms covered with brussels and plush carpets and rugs of such richness and beauty as quite bewildered me. The upholstery of the lounge chairs and other furniture I knew no name for was exquisitely enchanting and not calculated to make me feel much at home. The chief was very talkative and with Father continued their conversation far into the night.[7] We continued our course next morning

[5] See Chap. 1, n. 10.

[6] Situated three miles southeast of present-day Tahlequah, Oklahoma, Park Hill had been settled as early as 1829 by Old Settler Cherokees. Samuel Worcester, the venerable American Board missionary, made the settlement the site of his station and print shop in 1836. With the arrival of the Eastern Cherokees two years later, Park Hill became the site of the residences of John and Lewis Ross and George M. Murrell, a successful white merchant who was the son-in-law of Lewis Ross. The Cherokee Female Seminary was also located near the settlement. Of the buildings that so impressed Grayson only the Murrell Mansion survived to the present. See Carolyn T. Foreman, *Park Hill*, 5, 10, 50.

[7] John Ross built his home, Rose Cottage, in 1844, to which later that year he brought his 18-year-old Quaker bride. Named for the roses that bordered the driveway to the house, it was a two-story, rectangular wood-frame structure with

crossing some beautifully clear streams of water and dining at
the home of John Jones, who in the character of a Christian
Missionary had lived with the Cherokees for many years.[8]

Continuing our course I am not clear as to whether we
stopped over night again before reaching Fayetteville or not. I
only recollect that one evening we filed into that town riding
slowly along and looking at the houses and sign boards, appearing very much as if we were looking for something we had
lost and which we expected to find in some of the up-stair
windows along the side of the streets. Father always wore a
turban fashioned out of a shawl and this unique headgear
served to attract attention to us, as well as to emphasize our
uncouth appearance. Inquiring the way to the college we soon
reached it and met President Graham . . . [and] after having
considerable talk he referred us to a home nearby as a place
where we . . . [might] lodge over night. We found it to be the
home of an old Arkansas pioneer named McGarrah, who
while quite wealthy in land and city property, was coarse and
rough of manner, with very little if any school education, but
warm hearted and with all, hospitable.[9]

---

clapboard siding painted yellow. A gable roof, two external chimneys at either
end, and a recessed entryway behind four columns rendered it particularly im-
pressive. Ross was noted for his gracious hospitality to visitors of both high and
low rank. Rose Cottage was burned by Stand Watie's Confederate troops on Oct.
28, 1863. See Carolyn T. Foreman, *Park Hill*, 31, and Gary E. Moulton, *John
Ross: Cherokee Chief*, 143–44.

[8] John B. Jones was the son of the noted Baptist missionary Evan Jones, and
his residence was four miles north of present Westville, Oklahoma. At the very
time of the Graysons's visit, father and son were deeply involved in reestablishing
the Keetoowah Society among the Cherokees, a society of full bloods devoted to
retaining the traditions of the tribe and to the abolition of slavery. Supporters of
the Union, the Joneses fled the Cherokee Nation during the Civil War, but returned at the close of hostilities. John later served as U.S. agent of the Cherokees
from 1871 until his death in 1876. Morris L. Wardell, *A Political History of the
Cherokee Nation, 1838–1907*, 210n, 258; John Bartlett Meserve, "Chief Lewis
Downing and Chief Charles Thompson," *Chronicles of Oklahoma* 16 (Sept.,
1938): 325.

[9] In 1859 the population of Fayetteville did not exceed 673 whites and 294
blacks, and its commercial district numbered no more than two hotels and two
grocery stores. The college was located on ten tree-covered acres at the southeast
corner of Dickson and College streets. The principal building was a rectangular
two-story structure with clapboard siding painted white. The gable roof was

Remaining over night here we next morning repaired to the college grounds and buildings where my father talked some more with president Robert Graham, and turned me over to him. As Father did this and started to leave, I distinctly recall that his countenance changed and he came near yielding to his emotions—breaking down as we sometimes say—but controlled himself and left. Father had always been so stern, and at times severe toward me that I had come to thinking that perhaps he really did not have much or any parental affection for me, but this circumstance served to disabuse my mind of that conceit, and I was glad that I could now think otherwise. Parental control of children should be strict; obedience to the will and advice of the parent should be required and maintained; but the feeling of fear and dread of the parent should never be engendered in their tender minds, nor should any appearance of preference of one over other brothers and sisters be permitted to crop out in the actions of parents. If this last is permitted, it soon gives rise to a feeling of unfriendliness in the others for the favored child, and in the favorite a feeling of importance and fancied superiority that will do him no good.

After I had been taken in, the president arranged for my board and lodgings at the residence of Uncle Joe Lewis up in town, where I went and was received as a regular boarder, numbering with several other college boys who were already there.[10] I was now a duly initiated pupil of Arkansas College,

---

graced with a stepped cupola on the front, beneath which was an entry with sidelights. On either side were smaller square additions symmetrically placed and also with gable roofs, both of which were connected to the central buildings by enclosed walkways. William McGarrah, the previous owner of the school property, had surveyed the town in 1835 and owned one of the two grocery stores. See Donat, "Arkansas College," 1; Goodspeed, *History*, 236, 242–43.

[10] A member of a prominent merchant family, Joe Lewis had resided in Fayetteville since 1836 and attended the Christian Church with which the college was associated. President Graham left the college in Sept., 1859, to accept a teaching position with Kentucky University in Harrodsburg. He returned the following year, however, as a representative of the Christian Missionary Alliance. In 1862 he returned again to the Kentucky school, where he taught until 1896. He died in 1901 at the age of 80 years. See Goodspeed, *History*, 973–74, and Mary L. East, " 'Mr. Graham's School,' State's First College," *Arkansas Gazette*, Oct. 21, 1945, 1, 23.

an hundred or more miles from home, where everything was entirely different, and in most respects superior to anything I had ever seen or was accustomed to in the simple life I had hitherto led at my humble cabin homes in the forests of the Creek Nation, or the school at Asbury.

I was completely struck with awe and wonderment at my new surroundings. Here was a school where the pupils spoke not a word of Indian; scarcely a boy to be seen with jet black eyes and hair as were my late schoolmates at Asbury; their sports were different; their apparel [was] also different in material and make from mine. As I could clearly see, my uncouth appearance drew many eyes toward me to my sheer embarrassment. It was clear too that I was being regarded very much as [are] . . . children at the side shows of a circus, the ugly specimen of humanity said by the obliging manager to be the only living "Wild man of Borneo."

A feeling of loneliness came over me. A feeling as if I was completely isolated from the companionship of any one whom I might appeal to for sympathy or comfort possessed me, and for a time overpowered me. Going over to the spot where I last saw my father and cousin, I gave way to my feelings and shed a few tears. This was but for a moment, as I was fearful lest some of the boys might come up and observe my weakness of which I was ashamed. But it had been my ambition to come to Fayetteville to school and now that I was here, I was going to accommodate myself to the exigencies of my new environment and make the best of it. I saw and realized my verdancy and determined to let as little of it as possible appear in my actions to those with whom I was to associate. To this end I kept to myself and away from too near association with my school fellows, as I knew that in too free and easy commingling with them in sport or otherwise I was certain to be guilty of many breaches of the proprieties and expose my ignorance.

On the campus and elsewhere I did not endeavor to mix in the sports and pastimes engaged in by the boys but certain it is I was a close observer and student of everything that was going on around me. Occasionally a boy would approach and invite my participation in some game or exercise, or employ some of the arts known and used by boys to draw one another out, but all to no effect. I adhered to my plan to do or say nothing until I could feel that I was able to "do as Rome does." I "said nothing but sawed wood" until I felt myself fully able to conduct myself creditably in any of the activities that appeal to boys of my age at school on the grounds or elsewhere; but even then proceeded slowly and cautiously until in time I came to be identified with and active in most of the enterprises that engaged the attention of my associates. I have even to this day, looking back over the past, regarded this precaution above narrated, as a wise one, coming as it did from one of no more glowing antecedents.

When I entered this school there were in attendance already two Creek Indian boys, namely Wm.—Billy—McIntosh and Eli Jacobs. Later on another Indian, a Cherokee, the son of Stand Watie who was afterward general in the Confederate cause, named Saladen Watie, came and matriculated. I formed the acquaintance of McIntosh and Jacobs first of any of the scholars, but it was quite a good while before I could trust myself to be very sociable even with them, although they were of the same tribe of Indians with myself.

Having attended this school perhaps two months or more, I went to the general merchandise establishment of Messrs. Stirman and Dixon where I laid in for myself a suit of ready made clothing which I selected as I now recall with reference entirely to its adaptability to resistance of wear and tear, rather than its appeal to the requirements of the esthetic. Time passed on, however, and I became more civilized and more careful of my apparel and personal appearance, and thereafter had my clothing cut and sewed by the city tailor, and in the prevailing style.

I succeeded in obtaining a very good start in the studies taught at that time during this year's stay, and came home at the close of school and so well were my parents pleased with my general appearance and supposed advancement in the college course that when the school was again to be opened, they were quite willing and glad for me to return, although there was now much talk of war in the states. On my return to school

I know that I did not travel on horseback as when we went the year before, and just how I went is not now clear but I am of the opinion that I went to Van Buren where I took a stage coach which went direct to Fayetteville.[11]

This year was a profitable one for me, as I, along with the study of Arithmetic, English grammar and other elementary branches, took up Algebra, Latin grammar, and began the reading of Latin. I seemed to possess an aptitude for languages, and so marked was my proficiency in the Latin that some of my classmates expressed their firm belief that I studied the language when in school at home but was taking my place in a class of beginners where my former acquaintance with the study enabled me easily to lead the class. This, however, was not the fact at all, as it was absolutely true that I had never so much as seen a Latin book before becoming an inmate of this college, much less study one. In my other studies my standing and grade was only mediocre. I had now become well acquainted with the people and their ways and manners, and being freely accorded entree to some of the best families where I enjoyed the amenities and hospitality of the refined, I was in this way very much benefitted. I embraced the Christian church and was duly immersed by Joe Baxter.[12]

[11] The term ended in June, 1860. The new session began in September of that same year. Doubtless Grayson took the Butterfield Overland Stage, which had begun operations in late 1858. From Van Buren the stage went southwest through the Choctaw Nation into Texas and ultimately to California. It went northeast from Fayetteville into Missouri and then to Saint Louis. See Grant Foreman, "The California Overland Mail Route Through Oklahoma," *Chronicles of Oklahoma* 9 (Sept., 1931): 300–317, and Muriel H. Wright, "The Butterfield Overland Mail One Hundred Years Ago," *Chronicles of Oklahoma* 35 (Spring, 1957): 55–71.

[12] There is no Joe Baxter listed in the 1860 national census as living in Fayetteville. Probably the reference here should have been to William Baxter, who succeeded Robert Graham as president of Arkansas College in Sept., 1859. Also a native of England and a graduate of Bethany College, Baxter, who was a noted author and preacher, headed the school during its last days. A Union sympathizer during the Civil War, he remained in Fayetteville until early in 1863, when he fled to southern Ohio, there to continue his ministry and to write an account of the battles of Pea Ridge and Prairie Grove and their impact upon Arkansas College. See East, " 'Mr. Graham's School,' " 2.

Although Grayson "embraced" the Christian Church, he did not maintain that affiliation. Just when it is not clear, but later he identified with the Baptist Church

The talk of war between the North and South, however, was waxing continually greater, and before the session was out, if my present recollection serves me correctly, the school was thereby forced to set a day when it would close its doors for the present.[13] A short time before that day arrived I took passage on one of the stage coaches plying then between the small towns, for Van Buren whence I expected to find friends with conveyance to enable me to reach my home. The stage coach failed to make schedule time and was a day or more behind time, and when I reached Van Buren I learned that my brother Sam and a hired man had been sent to meet me but failing to join me, waited I think a day or two, and returned home. How I got conveyance from here, or how I traveled, or with whom, I have now no recollection, but know that after resting a day or two from the very tiresome ride in the great rolling and rocking old stage coach, I was at my home on the big public road from Ft. Gibson and North Fork to Texas, hereintofore mentioned.

I found that my parents had been in much distress of mind over the return of my brother and the hired man without me. [They felt] in their simple way that I was now lost to them for good and one or the other was disposed now to blame the other for ever having in the first place given consent for the nation to send me so far away from home. For them, therefore, my arrival was one of the happiest occasions of their lives, and for a time we were all happy; they, because the erstwhile absent and lost was found, and I, because I had rejoined my loved ones at the old home.

After living at home for a few days, however, my joy gave way to a very distressing loneliness and dissatisfaction. . . . [T]his sudden change from a life in a fairly good business town

and frequently attended and represented Creek Baptist congregations at denominational conferences. See Certificate of Appointment as Delegate to General Convention, Eufaula, May 1, 1888, File VIII-4, Box G-23, Grayson Family Papers, Western History Collections, University of Oklahoma.

[13] Arkansas College terminated its last academic session in March, 1861. The college building was burned in the aftermath of the battle of Pea Ridge on March 4, 1862, by retreating Confederate troops commanded by Gen. Benjamin Mc-Culloch. William Baxter, *Pea Ridge and Prairie Grove*, 29ff.

where many well dressed people were to be seen at all times intermingling with each other in trade or otherwise, to my humble cabin home in the quiet forests where only an occasional dusty and tired traveler was seen to pass along the road, was anything but agreeable to my now changed tastes and way of seeing things. The thought of remaining permanently here in these quiet solitudes was distressing indeed. I felt as if it was impossible for me to live here and make this my permanent home. Father's health was delicate, and his negro slave Wilson having died sometime previously, the work of providing for the support of the family consisting now of himself, Mother, myself, Samuel, Pilot, Louisa, Malone and James, Jr., was weighing upon him heavily. It was manifestly clear that I must remain here rendering whatever aid I may toward providing for the livelihood of the family.

After a short time I obtained employment as salesman in the general merchandise store of Samuel Smith at North Fork town at, I think now, fifteen dollars and board per month. War was being talked of much in the country, but the war fever did not yet prevail here as it did in the states, and the country and its affairs was yet in its normal state. How long I remained with Smith I do not know. Father's health had declined rapidly, and on that account, I think it was, it was deemed best that I should return home and help to look after things. He had now been forced to take to his bed and was in a bad way, being afflicted with what the physicians designated *liver complaint.*

He was at times better and again worse, and while he lingered on in this way now bad and again better, I was offered the position of salesman in the mercantile establishment of S. S. Sanger in North Fork, which was a more extensive and pretentious concern than was Smith's. Father decided that as I could be of no relief to him in his illness by remaining at home but was sure of a salary while working in town which was a much needed help toward the support of the family, I [might] . . . go and take employment of the Sangers if I wished. Accordingly I accepted the position offered and went home, I think, from my work in town at the end of each week to see how Father was progressing.

Creek burying ground near Okemah, circa 1910. *Western History Collections, University of Oklahoma Library.*

Early one morning before I was out of bed at the store brother Sam rode up near to the window of my bed room and called. Although I felt sure of the character of his mission at so early an hour, I asked what he wanted. He informed me that Pa had died the evening before, [and] I hastened into my clothes and went out home. From the very indefinite term designated by the physicians as *liver complaint,* Father's malady developed into dropsy, and all parts of his body were swollen to double or more their normal size. I remember that it required an immense coffin to contain his remains.

CHAPTER FOUR

Off to the Wars

BY THE TIME [my father had died the] war between the North and South which had been so long threatened had broken out and the gun-play was on. Quite all of the able bodied men capable of bearing arms throughout the country were enthusiastically enlisting in some one of the many military organizations that were being formed, and going from their homes into military encampments.[1] Although completely captivated by the glowing reports of the excitement, the novelty and other

[1] Military conflict between the northern and southern states began at Fort Sumpter, South Carolina, April, 12, 1861. Before that date, however, agents from Arkansas and Texas had converged upon the tribes of Indian Territory to persuade them to make common cause with the Confederate States of America. Representatives of the tribes met at North Fork Town, where Grayson was clerking, on July 1, 1861, and organized the "United Nations of the Indian Territory," and shortly thereafter they signed treaties negotiated with Confederate Commissioner Albert Pike. Ratified on July 20 by a council, the treaty with the Creeks divided the tribespeople into "Southern" and "Loyal" factions of almost equal numbers. The former were led by the chiefs Moty Kennard, who was Grayson's kinsman, and Echo Harjo, as well as Chilly and D. N. McIntosh. The latter, who were largely full bloods and principally identified with the Upper Towns, were led by Opothleyaholo and Sands. Related to and supported by Grayson's family, the Southern Creeks organized into a Confederate regiment, under Col. D. N. McIntosh; a battalion, under Lt. Col. Chilly McIntosh; and an independent company, under Capt. James M. C. Smith. These troops were initially attached to the Department of Indian Territory commanded by Col. Douglas H. Cooper in the absence of Gen. Albert Pike. The Loyal Creeks, along with groups of similar sympathies from different tribes, collected in the western part of their nation and appealed to the Union government for protection. See Debo, *Road to Disappearance,* 142–150.

enchantments of the life of the soldier in camps and on duty, I ignored my boyish inclinations and declined to join the army. . . . [I could] not see how Mother and the children could possibly support themselves without my assistance who was the oldest of the flock, and now quite useful as a bread earner. Besides, the enlistments of men in this country were not for service beyond the Mississippi river at or near the seat of war, but were to be devoted to such military service as was necessary in the Indian Territory. And as the enemy was no where threatening the peace or safety of our territory, there seemed little need for us all to rush pell mell to arms as the people were doing.

I therefore held back for quite a while longer helping to look after the welfare of Mother and the children. [At the same time] those who at first enlisted with so much spirit and éclat began to show signs of tiring of the life of a soldier in camp and to declare that if they must bear that which they now discovered was a hardship, others now in their comfortable homes must get out too, enlist and bear their share of the hardships of war. In some quarters it was said—"Here is Wash Grayson who is a well educated young man, capable of making a useful soldier in the army as a commissioned officer or otherwise, and yet he declines to join the army. He should be made to take his place in one of the companies and do duty as others are doing." This kind of talk, besides occasional inuendos derogatory to my personal courage in case of a conflict of arms, determined me to enter the field and show my critics, if occasion offered, the stuff I was made of, even if it cost my life to make the exhibition.

Just when or where I enlisted has escaped my memory, but it was perhaps after the war had been in progress for nearly or quite a year. D. H. Cooper who was an ex-U.S. Indian Agent for the Choctaws, was the General in command of the Indian brigade composed of the soldiers of the Creeks, Cherokees, Choctaws, Chickasaws and Seminoles. [Cooper] had followed the retreating Creeks, who under Hu-pui-helth Ya-ho-la [Opothleyaholo] were hastening to join the Federals in the state of Kansas and had one or perhaps two engagements with them

without any important results. [There being no] . . . other of
the enemy . . . in menacing distance of us, there was really
not much to call into martial activity our spirit of patriotism.[2]

When it was known that I had decided to join the army,
there were those who soon began planning for a lieutenancy
for me in the company (K) of the 2d Creek regiment of which
I had determined to become a member. When it came to my
knowledge I discouraged the movement, and declined to come
in in any other grade than that of a private soldier. As such,
[I] took my place in the company which was composed of the
old neighbors of long acquaintance, the Okfuskeys who lived
east of my home and the Eufaulas living on the west.

My pride of manhood had been ruffled by the criticisms I
had heard of and the hints given out that I was slow to enlist
probably because of fear of the danger incident to hostile engagement with the enemy. It was my fixed determination to
prove to my detractors that I sought not the ease and immuni-
ties supposedly belonging to the position of a commissioned
officer. . . . [Instead I] was willing to take my place in the
ranks with the rest of the boys subject to all the duties and
hardships incident to the life of a private soldier. No one I
think understood my motives for declining to stand for an office when all that was required of me was to express my consent, but I was actuated as I clearly remember by the impulses
and considerations as above stated.[3]

[2]Although no official record has been located, Grayson probably enlisted in
late 1862 or early 1863 at the age of 19 or 20. Born in 1815, a native of Mississippi and a veteran of the Mexican-American War, Douglas H. Cooper was appointed agent of the Choctaws on June 1, 1853. Beginning his Civil War military
career as a colonel, he ended it as a brigadier general commanding all Confederate troops in Indian Territory, including those of the Five Civilized Tribes.
Cooper actually fought three engagements with the Loyal Indians: Round Mountain on Nov. 19, 1861, Chusto Talasah on Dec. 9, and Chustenalah on Dec. 25.
In these battles, which pushed Opothleyaholo and the Loyalists into Kansas, his
command included units under Colonel McIntosh. After the war Cooper made
his home at old Fort Washita and prosecuted Indian claims against the federal
government. He died in April, 1879. Muriel H. Wright, "General Douglas H.
Cooper, C.S.A," *Chronicles of Oklahoma* 32 (Summer, 1954): 142–84.

[3]It was common practice for members of a military unit to elect lower-grade
officers. This tradition, incidentally, did not extend to Loyal Creeks who served
in Union forces.

How long I served as a private soldier in Co. K, 2d Creek regiment I do not know, but the need of my services, especially in view of my supposed superior education and fitness and ability, in the conduct of the affairs of our company was pressing. And discussion of the proposition to elevate me from the ranks to some official position wherein my services might be utilized in other more elevated spheres than that of guard and picket duty for the company continued; and over which I confess to a secret feeling of triumph and satisfaction. How I came to yield to these continued earnest solicitations I do not recall, for I rather enjoyed them, but suspect that the emoluments of the office, which would enable me to spare more pecuniary aid to my mother and the children at home, whom I never forgot, was perhaps the principal cause. Anyhow, I consented and was given the first lieutenancy of our company, in which office I served until by the death of our captain some time later I was promoted to that vacancy, and as capt. of Co. K. served to the close of the war. Having in years not yet attained my majority, I was a mere boy, and by far the youngest captain serving in the Indian brigade.

The first time that I with my company came any where near taking part in a scrap with the enemy, as I now recall, was at the battle of Honey Springs some two or three miles north of the present town of Checotah. We had been encamped in the vicinity of the Springs for some weeks when the enemy under Gen. Blunt came out of Fort Gibson to see what we were doing, and incidentally to feel our pulse if advisable. By what I have always confidently believed to be bad management, we lost the day here when the enemy came up and engaged us, for our Gen. Cooper did not even get all his men out on the firing line, or into any engagement with his adversary before he ordered his forces to retire.[4]

---

[4] The battle of Honey Springs occurred on July 17, 1863, on the site of the present community of Okatah along the eastern border of the old Creek Nation. Douglas Cooper, commanding approximately 6,000 troops, including units of all of the Five Tribes and a Texas Cavalry squadron, had moved north along the Texas Road, intending to attack Fort Gibson. When Cooper paused at Honey Springs to await reinforcements from Fort Smith, Arkansas, Gen. James G. Blunt, Union commander at Fort Gibson, unexpectedly led some 3,000 troops

With my own men and a picked body of others from the 2d
Creek regiment, with our colonel Chilly McIntosh in immediate command, we were ordered to occupy a certain position in
a dense bottom of the creek, and to remain out of sight under
cover of the foliage of the trees until ordered to take active
part in the day's work.[5] Here we remained listening breath-
lessly at the rattle of small arms and an occasional exulting
whoop that was one of the characteristics of the fighters of the
southern forces, and anxious to take a hand in the affray, but
could do nothing without orders. The morale of our men was
the best, and they could and would have made things alarm-
ingly unpleasant for whomever they might be pitted against.

On this occasion I remember hearing delivered by our colonel in Indian the finest war-speech I ever heard. Among other
things said by him in [the] course of his talk in which the men
were urged when the time came to do their full duty fearlessly
and bravely, [was]

---

against the Confederate positions. The First and Second Creek Regiments commanded by D. N. McIntosh, occupied Cooper's far left flank and were arrayed
along the upper crossing (the third above the bridge) on Elk Creek, just north of
Honey Springs, and they were facing federal units of the Third Wisconsin. Blam-
ing bad Mexican ammunition and enemy artillery superiority, Cooper abandoned
his position after a sharp morning battle that left 134 of his men killed or
wounded, and he retreated eastward as if to circle his adversary and hit Fort
Gibson in Blunt's absence. The Union general promptly returned to Gibson,
while Cooper set up his headquarters across the Canadian River from North Fork
Town. See Gen. Douglas H. Cooper, Imochia Creek, to Gen. William Steele,
Aug. 12, 1863, in *The War of the Rebellion: A Compilation of the Official Records of the Union and Confederate Armies* (hereinafter, *Official Records*), ser. i,
vol. 22, pt. 1, 457–62; Larry C. Rampp and Donald L. Rampp, *The Civil War
in the Indian Territory,* 23; and Grant Foreman, *Lore and Lure of Eastern Oklahoma,* 67–69.

⁵The eldest son of William McIntosh and the older brother of Daniel N.,
Chilly was born in the Coweta town in Alabama. He signed the infamous Treaty
of Indian Springs in 1825, but unlike his father he escaped execution by warriors
from the Upper Towns. Two years later he brought the first contingent of the
"McIntosh faction" to what is now Oklahoma, settling initially in the Verdigris
River valley. In addition to his support of southern secession and a Creek alliance
with the Confederacy, Chilly represented the tribe in a host of diplomatic negotiations before and after the war. He also was a talented Baptist minister. Chilly
died in 1875 at his home near present-day Fame in northern McIntosh County.
See John Bartlett Meserve, "The MacIntoshes," *Chronicles of Oklahoma* 10
(Sept., 1932): 318, 320, 323.

When you first saw the light, it was said of you "a man child is born." You must prove today whether or not this saying of you was true. The sun that hangs over our heads has no death, no end of days. It will continue indefinitely to rise and to set; but with you it is different. Man must die sometime, and since he must die, he can find no nobler death than that which overtakes him while fighting for his home, his fires and his country.

While awaiting orders for a forward move, here came orders for us to fall back and retire in good order, which reluctantly our men did. The good order of our retirement was perfect since there was no enemy or other thing in sight to cause disorder to our movements. This fiasco I think was the nearest I had up to that time ever come to being engaged in a battle with the enemy. A short time after this Gen. Blunt emboldened by his success at Honey Springs came into the Creek and Cherokee nations with a force of some 6000 men and scouted about the country near Briar Town and North Fork town. Cooper's forces retired south by way of the main public roads leading to Texas leaving the country to the enemy.[6]

[The Confederate retreat left] the families resident in the country . . . without any protection. And as the enemy was destroying everything in the way of their march, it was important that each family and non-combatant decide, and that quickly, whether to remain at home and trust to the mercy of the invading enemy, with whom they would probably be forced to go as they returned to Fort Gibson on the completion of the raid, or load up such few things as they were compelled to have, into wagons, and as our forces were doing, follow in retreat toward the Choctaw nation. Many were leaving practically all of their possessions, and loading up a few articles of

[6]General Cooper recrossed the Canadian River into the Creek Nation on July 22, 1863, intending to confront General Blunt again. He was defeated one more time at Prairie Springs, some 15 miles southeast of Fort Gibson across the Arkansas River. This time on his retreat southward he did not stop at the Canadian River. Blunt's forces probably numbered only 4,500 men. Briartown was in the Cherokee Nation on the north side of the Canadian River some 20 miles east of North Fork Town. At the latter location the Confederates had stored a large quantity of commissary supplies. See Foreman, *Lore and Lure*, 69, and Cooper to Steele, Aug. 12, 1863, *Official Records*, ser. i, vol. 22, pt. 1, 457–62.

bedding groceries and cooking utensils and following the retreating Confederate Army, while some had grimly decided to
stay at home with their stuff, trusting to the mercy of the
enemy when he shall come.

From our now retreating army I came home and found that
my relatives who mostly lived on the south side of the Canadian river had determined to take what few things they could
in wagons and go south. The question what we as a family
were to do must now be decided, and that in a hurry. The idea
of loading into one small ox wagon a few supplies and groceries that would last but a very few weeks at most, and starting
out with a mother and four helpless children, appeared to be
going right into a state of starvation and ruin. Mother declared
that her larger boys, Sam, Pilot and myself, [could] . . . go
with the retreating families, but that she with the younger children would remain as some other families were doing, at home
in the hope of being spared by the enemy when he came.

I remember that I favored her suggestion. Little Malone,
who was only a small boy, cried and said when the enemy
came and killed him it would hurt, and he was afraid to stay.
Here was where Sam Grayson came in and declared he thought
we could *pull through* if anybody else did, or words to that
effect, and that he was willing to try it, gloomy as appeared
the outlook. I have always accorded to Sam the honor and
praise I feel justly due to him for this decision which resulted
in holding our family together and preventing the separation
agreed on by Mother and myself which we afterward knew
would have been most disastrous. As I would be forced to
return and remain with my company and would not be able to
render aid in keeping our fleeing family out of the reach of the
pursuing enemy, and all the responsibility and work would de-
volve upon Sam, it seemed to me useless to hope for success
in flight. . . . But as Sam . . . was willing to brave the diffi-
culties and hardships we knew to be involved in the undertaking, we acquiesced in his decision. [After] loading up a few
articles of bedding and other absolutely needful things in the
wagon and hitching up, or rather yoking up, "Dave" and
"Ned," our faithful and only team to the wagon, [and with]

Pilot Grayson, brother of G. W. Grayson, circa 1892. Reproduced from
H. F. and E. S. O'Beirne, *The Indian Territory: Its Chiefs, Legislators, and
Leading Men.*

some of our party piling into the wagon and others on horses,
we hastily and mournfully prepared to leave our humble home
together with practically all of our little accumulations of
years.

The party was to drive across the Canadian river and join

Grandmother's and uncle Watt Grayson's moving party, which as we thought would not begin the exodus for a day or two. [Mean]while I would return to my company, see what general orders from our army headquarters were, and if I could, return and join Mother and the children and report as to the movement of our army and other people in the Creek nation. I went as planned to seek my company and regiment, but found the whole command more or less dispersed throughout the country, each man of family being absorbed with considerations for the safety and removal south of his women and children. I, on discovering this state of affairs, hastened back to join the movers at Grandmother's across the Canadian river, but arrived there in time only to find the place deserted. Our people had taken an additional alarm and left some two days earlier for farther south over some of the rockiest and roughest roads in that entire country.[7]

I had some acquaintance with the road over which our people had gone, and being well mounted followed in their wake fully expecting to overtake them. I had gone perhaps three miles or more from my grandmother's deserted plantation when I was overtaken in the mountains by a Mr. Washington, a clerk in the quartermaster general's office of our brigade. He appeared to me to be my senior by some two or three years, as I would judge, was a lone horseman, had in some way got cut off from the command in the mix-up over in the Creek nation, was trying to find it, but had no knowledge of the roads, the country or woodcraft. As I too was seeking the whereabouts of the same brigade, he suggested, if agreeable to become my traveling mate. While my preference was to travel alone, I had no excuses to urge against his becoming my traveling companion, except that he was a blond—blond hair, eye lashes, moustache and gray eyes, in fact blond all over. I cannot explain why, but I am not partial toward, but on the contrary have to confess to having always as now rather a repugnance to blonds of all degrees. But as this idiosyncrasy

[7] Probably this route twisted through the highlands east of Gaines Creek, now the south arm of Lake Eufaula, in northern Pittsburg County, Oklahoma.

would seem trivial and insensate to urge in this case. . . , I accepted his offer and we rode on together.

We [soon discovered] . . . that a detachment of the enemy had hastily pushed southward over a road leading from Ft. Smith toward Perryville and was now some where between us and the moving families I was trying to overtake.[8] Intersecting this road, we saw fresh signs indicating that the main body had only an hour or two previously passed on in the direction we were heading. We had to travel this same road however, but decided that it was a risky piece of business, as there might be stragglers along the route who might overtake us, or we might overtake them, and by them be roughly treated, especially since all the arms of defense we could muster between us consisted of one small revolver.

As we were riding along discussing the situation, we reached a small Choctaw farm of probably not over ten acres in extent on our right, planted in corn. As we rode silently along I observed ahead of us horses which appeared to be tied to the fence. We saw at first no riders although the horses were saddled and bridled. We halted and listened for the sound of voices but heard none. We then stealthily crept nearer when we saw, I think, two men lying near up to the fence fast asleep. My blond friend seemed to think this was our time to get in our work on the enemy and suggested that we rush upon and despatch them while they slept, and drew his revolver for this purpose. He had already impressed me as being not very practical in some of his ideas and views, and fearing he might be depending on the certain operation of his little old pistol, which might fail to work when we reached the despatching moment and cause us to be killed or taken prisoners, I asked to examine his gun. At a glance I became satisfied that there

[8]The reference here is to what was known as the California Trail, surveyed by Randolph B. Marcy in 1849, which followed along the southern highlands of the Canadian River across what is now Oklahoma. It intersected the Texas Road near present-day McAlester. Perryville, named for James Perry and situated five miles southwest of McAlester, was an important settlement and stage stop on the Texas Road. It was also connected with the California Trail both to the north and to the west. See Wright, "The Butterfield Overland Mail," map facing p. 60.

was great danger that it would not fire at all, and a wise view of the situation manifestly dictated that we go slow in this proposed work of death. The gun had never been shot for many months, and was so corroded that its cylinder would not yield to the effort of the hand to revolve it, much less revolve by the operation of its own mechanism.

We had no clubs at hand with which we might club them to death, and I was not sure that my blond friend and I were able to pounce upon these men and choke them to death. I counseled that we leave them to the continued enjoyment of their slumbers while we turned out into the woods, continuing our course but not traveling the roads. My woodcraft stood me in good hand here, and after touring the woods to a safe distance from the road, we examined more closely our only gun and found that it would not explode the charges contained in its cylinder, and in an engagement with an antagonist would not have been of near so much use as any well selected club. Seeing this my blond friend declared that it was a wise stroke of policy when I counseled that we move on leaving our enemy to the enjoyment of their dreams.

For many hours [we continued] our course through the mountains which because of the rocks and ravines rendered our progress necessarily slow and tedious. The day at length being far spent we sought out a proper lookout, whence we observed away below us a considerable prairie traversed by the road the enemy had traveled, and which we also desired to travel but dared not attempt. I determined to go down to this road where we could see the enemy for a long distance if he was in sight, any where in the front or rear of us, and travel it in safety until forced to leave it. We soon reached the road and found that a considerable force of the enemy had just passed ahead of us but were no where in sight.

While we were riding tiresomely along this dusty road we saw two men we took to be the enemy riding our way. They were coming at a fast gallop when we, unmindful of possible ditches and gullies that might be hidden in the luxurious grass where in the distance everything appeared smooth and level, broke away from the road toward the timbered hills and mountains to the southeast in a faster gait. Unexpectedly to me my horse ran squarely up to a gully of considerable width and depth but fortunately for me cleared it at one leap without so much as a halt. My blond friend, who I think was some distance behind, seeing the leap my horse made, had time to steer clear of the gully and was saved the trouble of making the somewhat dangerous leap. We got into the timber and rode on into the . . . mountains, by which time it was quite dark.

Feeling safe from any possible pursuers we unsaddled our now much jaded horses, and lariating them out on the grass which was in luxurious abundance every where about us, with our sweaty saddle blankets for a bed and saddles for pillows, we laid us down to sleep. Tired as we were, we were still talking over our experience of the day when we heard what sounded much like the firing of a cannon. We heard the sound repeated several times a little south of west of where we stood. We knew that this must be a result of a meeting of the enemy whom we had all day been avoiding, with our comrades under Gen. Cooper somewhere in the vicinity of, if not at, the little town of Perryville. Lest some scouting party be sent out from this night battle who might discover our roosting place in these mountains and disturb our rest before day, we saddled up our horses and again moved higher up, this time among the crags where we thought none could molest or "make us afraid" where we again spread our pallet as before and slept without a disturbing dream or nightmare, being too tired and hungry for either, until morning.[9]

[9]Grayson and his companion were apparently in the highlands just north of present-day Krebs when they heard the cannons associated with the battle of Perryville on the evening of Aug. 26, 1863. The 9,000 Confederates under Generals Cooper and William Steele had retreated south along the Texas Road, leaving behind at Perryville a rear guard to delay the 4,500 Union troops in General Blunt's command. After a brief engagement Union forces entered Perryville and burned the entire community with its large store of Confederate supplies. Cooper and Steele continued their southward retreat to Boggy Depot in present-day western Atoka County; Col. D. N. McIntosh and his Creek regiments turned to the

I had now lost all trail of the fleeing refugees with whom Mother and the children were traveling. [There was] no way of ever hearing or learning of them save by making my way to wherever the Creeks were refugeeing in the Choctaw Nation and finding them there or learning of their capture. But with the trail lost, the enemy between me and them, and the experience of yesterday and last night, I knew it was highly probable, indeed almost certain, that the entire party had been overtaken and captured, they being unable with their slow and unwieldy ox teams and wagons to keep out of the enemy's way. This course of reasoning dispelled the hope I had of coming up with Mother and the children somewhere while they were yet in flight, and brought over me a feeling of melancholy sadness that worried me. Still there was but one thing to do—press on south keeping out of the way of the enemy until I could reach our lines and there obtain tidings if possible of the missing families.

So the next morning my friend and I continued our course under my guidance, describing a detour that left out of our way all of that country environing the town of Perryville where we were satisfied occurred the disturbance of last night. A day or two after this, we rode into the headquarters of our brigade, which if I am not mistaken, was encamped on one of the streams of the Choctaw nation known as the Boggies.[10] Being

---

west; and Arkansas troops under Gen. William Cabell fled to Fort Smith. Blunt followed the latter, and on Sept. 1, 1863, he seized the Arkansas post without a battle. By September, therefore, Union forces controlled the area north of the Canadian and Arkansas rivers and were preparing to push south to Red River. James G. Blunt, Perryville, to John M. Schofield, Aug. 27, 1863, *Official Records*, ser. i, vol. 22, pt. 1, 5977–98; and Rampp and Rampp, *Civil War in the Indian Territory*, 32–34.

[10]Principally draining present-day Coal and Atoka counties, the Muddy, Clear, and North Boggy creeks flow southeast to the Red River. Correspondence from General Steele places the Confederate encampment on "Little" Boggy, which probably was Clear Boggy Creek. Where the latter intersected with the Texas Road and Butterfield Stage Route, the settlement of Boggy Depot flourished after it was established in the 1830s. It was a post office after 1850, and for a few months in 1858 was the capitol of the Choctaw Nation. During the Civil War, Boggy Depot was also an important resupply post for the Confederacy. Prob-

the last ones from within the late lines of the enemy, the general was naturally anxious to learn what news we brought. At this date . . . I am not positive that we appeared before the commanding general, D. H. Cooper, but am of the impression that we reported to some other officer—the adjutant general perhaps. In the matter of rendering of this report, I remember distinctly that to me it was quite striking. Perhaps because of his seniority, or more likely, his personal acquaintance with the officers at headquarters, some of whom seemed to know him personally, my blond friend, now somewhat bronzed by his exposure to the atmosphere outside of the quartermaster general's tent, gladly took the lead in satisfying the inquiring ones.

Since I am writing of myself not for publication but for the information of my family only, I must here make a confession which ordinarily I would not. In the experiences of the last few days past, I was unable to regard myself in any other light than as the guiding spirit of our actions and movements; the one whose foresight, watchfulness and knowledge of practical woodcraft in general had kept us from being picked up by the enemy, and who had at last succeeded in picking our way safely into the friendly camps of our comrades and friends. I was a good woodsman for my age, a much needed qualification in one traveling in the woods and avoiding roads; could keep in mind the cardinal points of the compass wherever I was; was resourceful and apt in meeting the exigencies arising from unforeseen conditions and inured to hardships; while my companion who was indeed a very nice gentleman and quite accomplished in many other respects, seemed to lack in a remarkable degree these commonplace qualifications, and in these circumstances greatly needed just such a leader and counselor as I had been. When therefore he came to narrating our experiences and observations of the past several days to the military authorities, and told the story as if he had been the guiding genius and the undaunted hero who surmounted all obstacles, and as if he might have been *alone* and I not in it, I could not help noticing what appeared to me an unfair way of telling the story but, of course said nothing until now.

I have no recollection of ever having met my friend any time after this, and as he was, as I think, a few years my senior, it is of course quite likely that he has passed over to the other side. He was a very good man with, I think, many more good qualities of heart and brain than bad ones, which is evident from the position he occupied in the cause we were both serving. If dead, peace to his ashes; if alive still, abundant success to comrade Washington.

CHAPTER FIVE

Life of a Soldier

To MY AGREEABLE SURPRISE, [upon regaining friendly lines I learned] our fleeing families had not been overtaken and captured by the enemy but were safe and sound in camps near Wah-pah-nah-ke academy in the Chickasaw Nation. . . .[1] After our women and children were located and temporarily provided for, all the soldier members of the families were ordered to repair to a military encampment that was then forming, whence they would return toward the enemy's lines, the South Canadian river being considered the dividing boundary line between us. The companies having gotten into shape for military duty, a scout of some one or two hundred men, with instructions to go as far north of the Canadian river and ascertain if possible where the enemy was, and see what damage had been done to the country in the last raid, was despatched. With these I went.

[1] Located 2½ miles southeast of Bromide in present-day Johnston County, and some ten miles west of Boggy Depot, Wapanucka Academy was a school for girls opened by the Chickasaws in 1852 and administered by the General Assembly of the Presbyterian Church. The principal building was a large, three-story, rectangular rock structure with a gable roof and interior chimneys at either end. A two-story extension at one end, with another chimney and double verandas along the front and back, gave the structure almost a Georgian look. See Muriel H. Wright, "Wapanucka Academy, Chickasaw Nation," *Chronicles of Oklahoma* 12 (Dec., 1934): 402–31.

We reached and crossed the river a considerable distance above the Creek settlement formerly known as Hillabee.[2] [As] our column . . . [moved] down the river and through the above settlement, evidences of the devastation visited by the enemy in his late raid . . . [were] visible on all sides with here and there a hastily made grave to be seen along the road. At about sun down we reached one home where the family . . . [was] still residing, being by reason of illness, unable to go anywhere. A daughter of Dick Benson, her sick husband and some others, were living here. Some of them ran away from the house to the thickets nearby on the approach of our advance but returned when informed of whom we were.

The Bensons being related to me as stated in the earlier part of these writings, I lingered some few minutes talking to the family after our command had passed on and disappeared.[3] When I started away from the house to join my company, I soon found that they had traveled in such haste as to have got away beyond hearing distance. In the gathering gloom of twilight I was unable to follow their track, nor could I hear any noise they might make. In the fast fading twilight I could see many roads and paths but could not discern what one had been taken by the scouting party, look as closely as I may. Here I was alone with the enemy's lines and in the immediate neighborhood of where he had only a day or two since been and played much havoc, and [I had] foolishly allowed myself to lose the command that I had come into the country with, while darkness was upon me making the prospects that much the more gloomy. Where the scouting party was or where to hunt it I did not know.

I was in a fix. I was bothered, and in fact pretty well scared up. While riding along a path in the dark in this state of mind, I reached a spot where there was a slight opening in the underbrush that closely hugged my way on either side. I observed a gray appearing object lying some twenty or more feet west of

---

[2]Hillabee was located some 20 miles southwest of Eufaula just north of the Canadian River. It will be remembered that Grayson's paternal ancestors had settled among the Hillabees in the old Creek Nation.

[3]See Chap. 1, n. 12.

the path I was traveling. At first I mistook it for a piece of an old dry log five or six feet long that some wood chopper had left after cutting and removing the limbs and so much of the trunk as he wanted. Something about its appearance, however, was sufficiently noticeable to cause me to turn out of my way to examine it more closely. I found it to be the corpse of a man who presumably had fallen before the enemy's aim within the last day or two.

One can well imagine my feelings. My fears and imaginations were now thoroughly aroused and I quickly passed on in an easterly direction in the hope of eventually hearing the neigh of a horse or some slight noise made by the men of our command who must by now have gone into camp, which would lead me to our camps. In any case, I desired as soon as I could to get away as fast and as far as possible from this uncanny discovery back by the pathway.

While hastening along in this excitement and perturbation, I heard in the darkness ahead somebody coming on horse back meeting me. This might be a straggler from our scouting party but was quite as likely to be one of the enemy As I could hear the hoof sounds of but one horse, I determined to meet him be he friend or foe and risk the consequences. As he came within about fifty steps of me, I ordered him to halt and inform me whether he was friend or foe. "I am Bob Childers of the 1st Creek regiment; aren't you Capt. Grayson of the 2d Creeks?" A few words of explanation soon showed that he too had in some way become segregated from our scouting party and was unsuccessfully endeavoring to find them the same as I was.

I informed him of the unwelcome *find* I had made a few rods up the pathway. He suggested that we go back and see it, which we did. Childers and I, while not particular friends in the sense commonly conveyed by the terms, were acquaintances of quite long standing, he maintaining a good standing in his regiment as a reliable and successful scout.

There being now two of us together, we, each I think feeling relieved from the worry of the last hour or more—I am sure I did—left our dead man, and at once began planning for our own safety and rest during the night, which promised to be cold and frosty. To stop anywhere on the ridges and high grounds nearby and build up such a camp fire as was necessary to keep us near comfortably warm was too risky. The glare or light of our fire would attract the attention of the enemy if he was in camps anywhere nearby and cause him to run on to, surprise and relegate us to the happy hunting grounds as they had the fellow we left lying up by the road.

Yet we were bound to have a fire to keep us warm, so we repaired to the low and dark bottoms of the Me-o-kof-ko-tse, otherwise called Mill Creek.[4] [There] the light and glare of a camp fire could not be seen over the tops of the tall trees of the bottoms and attract the attention of any one even if comparatively near us. We did not proceed far in search for a suitable place to kindle this fire before we found a short way from the channel of the stream a large pile of driftwood and debris that had been brought down during a big rise in the stream sometime in the past when the waters exceeded the limits of the stream, which was dry and combustible. We set fire to this when the lighter debris blazed up immensely, lighting up the creek bottom for a long distance away, not much to our liking as we were very averse to building up a light that might attract the attention of the enemy whose whereabouts we suspected to be somewhere in the vicinity. This was soon consumed, however, leaving the large logs burning and affording us a comfortable camp fire during the entire night, which was very chilly.

The next morning we overtook our men . . . and with them scoured the country for the purpose if possible of locating the enemy. Finding that he had returned to headquarters in Fort Gibson north of the Arkansas river, we turned our course south toward our own headquarters on Mill Creek in the Chickasaw nation.[5] On this return trip the young horse I was riding became completely fagged out on the last day of our march,

[4]This stream empties into the Canadian River and is located in present-day McIntosh County southwest of Eufaula.

[5]Mill Creek flows through Johnston County northwest of Tishomingo and empties into the Washita River. It was approximately 100 miles southwest from Hillabee to Mill Creek.

when we were in a very mountainous and rough country within some ten or fifteen miles of our camps, toward which we were heading. Urge him as I would, I could not toward the last force him into any other gait than a slow walk with head and ears no more erect with life and spirit, but down cast with every indication so well understood by cavalrymen of distressing fatigue. One becomes greatly attached to any horse that he has had the exclusive use of for any considerable time, but especially fond and friendly becomes this attachment when he feels that his horse has on occasion been the means of helping him through, probably saved his life in many thrilling junctures and hair raising escapades. Especially in our cases was this so, as we all rode horses that were our private property.

I therefore could not find it in me to try to force my good horse and noble friend to keep pace with the march of my men when his strength was so nearly exhausted. I therefore directed my men to continue the march with the scout into camps while I would follow on as best I could and join them at our headquarters as soon as the jaded condition of my horse would permit. The men went on and I permitted my horse to take his own time and proceed to carry me at such gait as best befitted his condition, at which we proceeded until dark. We were in the mountains where the timber was heavy, the road exceedingly rocky, and being one I had never before traveled I knew not where I was, but only that I was in a lonely mountain ten or more miles away from any habitation of civilized men.

It had frequently been reported that the wolves of some of the mountains of the Chickasaw nation had attacked and killed lone travelers in the woods. It was well known too that panthers made these wilds their home. While passing along the rocky road in the darkness and solemn silence of these mountains, I could not help thinking of what I had heard told of these ferocious animals and what I and my horse would do in case of an attack by them. I had a good revolver and an abundant supply of ammunition and felt that I would be able in all probability to hold them off should they make an attack on me while I was awake. But it was now late in the night, and I was sleepy as I could well be, while my faithful horse was so hungry for food that he would every now and then reach out to the side of the road against my protest and nip a blade of grass or succulent plant. I had to have some sleep while my horse had to be lariated on the grass.

My fatigue was so great that when once asleep I was certain that my sleep would be so sound that the stealthy approach of wolf or panther would not awaken me until he had his fangs fastened in my vitals. I rode wearily along thinking therefore of the situation until I could hold out no longer and determined to stop and seek sleep and rest for myself and grass for my horse. I rode out to the east side of the road and found a tree with limbs reaching near the ground and which in case of necessity I could easily climb. At the base I deposited my saddle for a pillow and spreading down my saddle blanket for a pallet, and after lariating my horse to the same tree, tieing the rope only a few inches above my head, I consigned myself to dreamland. . . . The precaution of tying my horse to the same tree under which I slept was resorted to on the theory that in feeding on the grass about me he would circle around the tree during the night and thus by continually causing the rope with which he was tied to pass over my face and neck, so effectively disturb my sleep as that I would be about half awake all night, and thus be in perhaps a better condition to meet or escape any attack of panther or man-eating wolves.

This homely precaution I have never heard of any adopting, but it is certainly striking how when a man is brought face to face with dangers real or imaginary his brain will find and improvise expedients and ways and means to meet such emergencies. So my fear of harm and desire for self preservation caused me to resort to this peculiar plan which in the light of subsequent events seemed to have been unnecessary. No wolves or panthers molested me or my horse, morning dawned [and] I had a fairly good night's rest. My faithful horse being much rested and refreshed, we proceeded on our way and by the hour of ten or eleven o'clock the next morning we were within the hospitable camps of our friends. The experiences of this expedition were among my most trying ones of the war.

After resting up from the wear and tear of this expedition the army was ordered to make ready for a forward movement toward the front. After some days of preparation we moved from Mill Creek in a northeasterly course through the Choctaw Nation. After some days of leisurely movements we established our camps on a stream designated Brazeel [Brazil] where we remained for perhaps a week or more watching and annoying as much as possible the enemy occupying Fort Smith.[6]

While in these camps the men were permitted to go out in foraging parties and take from the farms as feed for their horses the corn which had never been gathered from the stalk as yet by the farmers of the country. On a certain pleasant autumn morning a number of my men as well as others, and myself, went up the mainroad leading to Ft. Smith to a small farm of some four or five acres situated on the west side of the road, some two miles from our camps, to obtain some corn that stood in it. The east string of fence of this enclosure extended its full length in a line parallel with the road with the gate or entrance opening on the road. When I reached the farm there were already men in it each gathering corn and caring for it as best he could, while others had gone on up the road in the direction of where the enemy was known to be prospecting for no telling what.[7]

Seeing that if I was to obtain any of this corn I should at once "get busy," I entered the field at the gateway and has-

[6] In the spring of 1864 the First and Second Creek Regiments were attached to the First Indian Cavalry Brigade commanded by Stand Watie. A Cherokee who early espoused the Confederate cause, Watie was the only Indian to achieve the rank of brigadier general in either of the contending armies. Ordered to challenge and watch federal forces at Fort Smith, he moved his troops along the Butterfield Overland Mail route to Brazil Creek in northwestern Leflore County to camps west of present-day Panama. See Kenny A. Franks, *Stand Watie and the Agony of the Cherokee Nation*, 160.

[7] Given the sequence of events subsequently narrated and extant evidence documenting the time frame, Grayson's memory failed him by placing this event in the context of "autumn" and field-dried corn. More than likely it occurred in May, 1864, if it took place just prior to the capture of the *J. R. Williams*. On the other hand, Grayson was on maneuvers in the Fort Smith area in August, 1864. The event described may have taken place then, although that too is still a bit early for "autumn." See Franks, *Stand Watie*, 160.

tened toward the west, the back side. I had succeeded in obtaining only a few ears when I heard several shots up the road, but that was a common thing and at first did not arrest my attention from my work in hand. But presently I heard one or two more shots, then others and finally many more accompanied with the yelling and whooping characteristic of our men in a fight. Looking toward the entrance where I came into the corn field, I observed my foraging party hustling through it as fast as possible and hastening back toward our camps as rapidly as horseflesh would carry them, throwing their recently gathered corn in every direction as they went.

By this time the pursuing enemy, [with] our flying scouts still exchanging shots, had gotten up to and were passing the entrance of the corn field in hot haste cutting me completely off from my retreating comrades, rendering egress by the way I had entered quite out of the question. Seeing this I rode to the fence on the back of the field and reaching over the head of my horse in a great hurry pushed on the rail fence expecting to raze it almost to the ground. To my surprise and alarm it refused to be demolished, and the best I could do was the throwing off of a few—about two—top rails. This done, I put spurs to my horse—Rover—who with a bound cleared it, alighting in very thick high weeds and brush.

Here was another surprise. There was only five or six feet of ground between the fence and a very steep bank—too nearly perpendicular for anyone to ride down, which when we made the leap, we could not see for the thick underbrush and weeds that concealed it from view. There was now no time to think and lay plans, so I indicated to Rover that he should carry me down that bluff, when he as readily made the effort to comply by making one step off and—well, he made no more, for we went down in double quick time, some fifteen or twenty feet after the fashion of a toboggan without the least impediment to arrest our slide until we stood in water up to my saddle. In my excitement supplemented by the thick brush, I had not the least suspicion of the existence of this bluff and creek until I was in it. It was no difficult matter, however, to ford the stream now that we were in it.

We soon reached the open bottoms on the opposite side from the field, where I defied any Federal scout to capture me. I rode some distance up the bottom away from the scene of my somewhat exciting experiences and finding some trees known as black haw loaded with ripe fruit, I put in a few minutes gathering and eating these while Rover luxuriated on the succulent growths of the bottoms. After some cogitations of the disadvantages of war and some of the funny things that I was fast finding were incident to the life of a warrior in time of general belligerency, I returned to camp. After remaining here some days longer without any other meeting with the enemy, the Indian brigade was ordered to take a position farther to the north and within easy reach of the Arkansas river. We, therefore, moved over and encamped on the Sans Bois.[8]

After a few days' halt, I was furnished with a detachment of three hundred men and a battery of light artillery and ordered to go and picket a certain point on the south banks of the Arkansas river known as Pleasant Bluffs. In earlier day [at Pleasant Bluffs there] flourished a trading post which in a limited way supplied the general merchandise for the people of the sparsely settled neighborhood, but which had long since been abandoned, with nothing remaining to mark the spot now but an old empty and dilapidated house.[9]

General Stand Watie who despatched me to this point ordered me to occupy the place at once and so dispose my guns on the banks of the river as to be concealed from, while [still] commanding, any possible passing craft as had been known lately to have passed loaded with supplies from Ft. Smith for the Federal forces at Fort Gibson, and stop and "take it in out of the wet" as it were. Outside of commanding my own com-

---

[8] Sans Bois Creek drains southern and eastern Haskell County before emptying into the Canadian River from the south. The camps were probably located in the vicinity of Keota.

[9] Pleasant Bluff was an historic landmark on the south bank of the Arkansas River six miles below its confluence with the Canadian. Thirteen miles northeast of present-day Stigler, and now almost inundated by Robert S. Kerr Reservoir, it was a major crossing and steamboat landing and, since the 1830s, the site of a Choctaw settlement known as Tamaha. Grayson occupied this position in early June, 1864. See Kent Ruth, *Oklahoma Travel Handbook*, 221.

pany, this was the first time that a detachment of other men had been placed under my charge, and considering my youth and inexperience, I felt a spirit of pride come over me that determined me to do my very best and prove myself worthy of the trust and confidence reposed in me by my superiors.

Reaching Pleasant Bluffs I encamped my men, and selected commanding positions for my artillery, I located and so masked the guns with the boughs of trees cut and positioned for that purpose that no enemy could see them. This done, I quietly awaited events and Gen. Watie, who was to follow soon with the main body of our force.

In a few days, during which nothing of interest occurred, the commanding general reached my camps with the reserve and looking over it and the emplacements selected and in which I had disposed of my guns, he expressed approval of everything I had done and never offered any changes whatever. This was another circumstance of which I was proud and have never forgotten. These were really unimportant circumstances, and in the estimation of many would not seem worthy of notice, but when it is remembered that I was then only a very young captain, only about nineteen (19) years of age, and with little or no experience in military affairs, I believe my mention of and pride in them will appear pardonable to the considerate.[10]

After the arrival of the general with the reserve, we remained in these camps for some three or four days watching and waiting, when one afternoon a passing boat of the enemy plying up the middle of the river and toward us—the very object we had come here to meet and if possible intercept and capture—came in sight. In a very few minutes we were in readiness for action and lined up on the banks of the river. When this craft was within easy reach of all of our artillery which we had strung out some hundreds of yards on the banks of the river, a harmless shot was fired across its bow, which as I was informed was a rule of war to warn the enemy of our presence and belligerent intentions and afford him an oppor-

[10] Actually, Grayson was 21 years old.

tunity to offer terms without a conflict if he so chose. In this case he did not choose.

We opened up on him in fine style and soon filled the air with the roar of cannon and rattle of small arms. An escort of twenty five men that was aboard fired one volley without effect, and jumping out of the now disabled boat into the water nearly waist deep, fled to the brush on the other side. The boat being now out of commission and helpless, the sign of surrender was waved from the pilot house when we ceased our attack and sent some three men, I think it was, to go and formally take possession, which they did. Although crippled, the engine and machinery was sufficiently intact to float it over on the side we were.

This done, a guard was placed over [the vessel] and an account taken of the damage done and the extent of the booty captured. The boiler had been punctured, the other machinery disabled, and one man killed. The Captain and pilot, the lieutenant—Houston by name, I think—who commanded the escort, one white and one negro woman were captured. The cargo consisted of a large quantity of hominy in barrels, dried and smoked salt pork and other groceries, and an extensive assortment of dry goods presumably for the sutlers of Fort Gibson. These were taken from the boat as soon as possible, when it was set on fire and pushed out into the current of the river, burning to the water's edge before floating over a mile thus, ending the usefulness of the *J. R. Williams,* which was the name of the craft.[11]

Gen. Watie had no means of transportation whereby might be transported these valuable goods, so we maintained a guard

[11] The engagement took place on June 15, 1864. Surprisingly, Stand Watie in his official report of the event failed to mention Grayson at all, noting instead that the three pieces of cannon were commanded by Lt. Forrester of Lee's light battery. He also recorded that there were four Union fatalities, that one of those captured was a black female, and that the booty included 150 barrels of flour, 16,000 pounds of bacon, and a considerable quantity of store goods. See Stand Watie, Pheasant Bluff and Limestone Prairie, to D. H. Cooper, June 17 and 27, 1864, *Official Records,* ser. i, vol. 34, pt. 1, 1012–13; and also Frank Cunningham, *General Stand Watie's Confederate Indians,* 143–44; and Wiley Britton, *The Union Indian Brigade in the Civil War,* 403–405.

over the stuff waiting to be furnished with army wagons by Gen. Cooper into which we could load and carry them to where they could be distributed to our needy army. The dry goods was distributed to our men.[12]

We had thus been waiting for several days when information was received that a body of the enemy from Ft. Smith was moving up to dispute with us our right to hold the booty we had captured. Here we were only a scout of some fifteen hundred men far away from our base, with light artillery of great value to our army. To jeopardize this as well as other interests only in the hope of saving a quantity of hominy and smoked salt pork was not wise military judgment. What we came to do had been successfully accomplished. It was therefore determined that we destroy the remainder of our capture and return to our base. Orders were given for the immediate destruction of the goods, when whatever the men could not carry away was soon seen ascending in flames and black smoke.[13]

General Watie called on the Creeks to furnish a sentinel of a suitable number of trusty men to remain and stand watch until *sun down* on the site of our present encampment after our forces had left the grounds in retreat, and in case the enemy appeared in pursuit, to hasten and overtake our retreating men and give the alarm. Orders came to me specifically to furnish these sentinels, after which orders were given for making ready and retiring. When it became known that we were to leave this evening in haste, the object mainly in view being the saving of our artillery from capture by the enemy now said to be moving up in force to try our strength by land, there certainly was activity in hot haste, every man running here and there getting himself in readiness for flight, fully determined not to be left behind in this get-away.

[12] As Grayson will later admit, Watie reported that he lost control of his forces and that a great many Creeks and Seminoles took their plunder and abandoned camp, leaving an insufficient force to protect the battery from an attack by federal forces. In addition to sources in n. 11 above, see Franks, *Stand Watie*, 162–63.

[13] For an extended discussion of the engagement at Pleasant Bluff, see Keun Sang Lee, "The Capture of the *J. R. Williams*," *Chronicles of Oklahoma* 55 (Spring, 1982): 22–38.

With the men in this state of alarm and perturbation and the well known lack of discipline in our ranks, I was fully aware that I had no ghost of a chance to succeed in obtaining from among them such sentinels as were required of me. I made the effort, however, and, as I had expected, I failed to get a single man to remain. I was sorry and ashamed of my Creek soldiers. I, a Creek, had been the first to be sent here to picket the place with men and artillery and had made good; and now when it . . . [was] necessary to have men to stand watch at this place for only a few hours for the expected approach of the enemy in pursuit, while our forces retreated in safety with our victorious guns and other valuable properties, I am further honored with the responsibility of furnishing the men to fill the rather dangerous post. This bespoke confidence in the Creeks and me, and I regarded the circumstance as a credit and appreciation of our worth that we could not afford to ignore.

Too proud to report back that I could not find a man in my command who would join in picketing the post, I determined that the Creeks should not fall down (fail) on this last call to duty no matter what the cost may be. I knew of one Creek who could and would prevent such a failure being charged up against the courage and manhood of his tribe in time of war. The Creeks fail now? Fail when failure meant so much to their discredit and to the safety of our retiring troops? No! By the eternal no! I . . . [would] personally assume the responsibility of watching this point, and of giving warning to our retiring troops in case of the approach of the enemy. This was as much as ten or more men could do and all the commanding general required, and I would do it, and it . . . [should] never be known that at this juncture of our affairs at Pleasant Bluffs there was any dearth of men to stand watch when such service was called for and regarded as a dangerous one.

Few if any suspected the contending emotions occupying my disturbed mind. Preserving a placid mien, however, I delivered a few simple instructions to my men and further informed them that I would not march just now but would overtake them later. My company being K, [it] was always the rear one in a line of march, and on this evening they being now ready to move, stood in line while our artillery and all the baggage and ammunition wagons and all the other companies filed by. They took their place in the line of march and soon our whole force was out of sight, leaving our erstwhile animated camp to approaching "darkness and to me." [14] In a few minutes the scene of bustle and life of a few hours ago was as quiet as a grave yard. The clatter in the distance of the army wagons and caissons over the rough road, which for a time seemed to keep me company and in some way maintained my connection with our forces, soon died completely out, filling me with a solemn loneliness and dread that led me instinctively to look to the west to observe how near the sun was to sinking below the horizon, but this was still considerably in the future.

On the prairie south of me stood a small bald elevation that may be properly designated as a mount, on which our general desired that I station the watchmen. To this I slowly and quietly made my way, and reaching its highest point, took my lonely stand in the almost oppressive silence of the on-coming but to me, too poky sun set, feeling myself the none-too willing "monarch of all I surveyed." [15] My instructions were for my watchmen to hold the position if not disturbed until *sun down;* and this I had undertaken singly and alone to do, and unless forced away by a hostile force, I certainly would carry these instructions out to the letter. The phrase *sun down* was upper-most in my mind all the while. I rode from one spot to another, [getting] . . . down from my horse[;] but this was risky business and I would immediately vault back into the saddle.

How fearfully slow the minutes passed! *Sun down!* When . . . [would] that moment come! Not to be caught unawares, my eyes I kept constantly sweeping the horizon in all

---

[14]The Confederates withdrew from Pleasant Bluff on June 18 or 19, 1864. See Rampp and Rampp, *Civil War in the Indian Territory,* 87–88. "Darkness and to me" is a quotation from Thomas Gray's "Elegy Written in a Country Churchyard." *The Oxford Dictionary of Quotations,* 2d ed. (New York and London: Oxford University Press, 1959), 229 (28).

[15]Grayson quotes here from William Cowper's "Verses Supposed to be Written by Alexander Selkirk." See *The Oxford Dictionary of Quotations,* 164 (22).

directions and especially toward the slowly sinking sun. The fact is that I feared I was in great danger and was exceedingly anxious to be moving away from this place of danger, but was determined not to go until the time fixed had fully expired. I looked and looked, but saw no enemy, nor did the sun go down. The awe-inspiring silence prevailing in depressing supremacy all around . . . [was] only broken now by the chirp of a lonely cricket,

> And all the air a solemn stillness holds
> Save where the beetle wheels his droning flight

rending the stillness all the more acute and depressive.[16] I patted my horse on the neck, talked familiarly to him as if he understood my words and in other ways tried to divert my thoughts of possible dangers that might overtake me in the next few minutes consequent upon my almost fanatical determination to carry out my instructions to the letter.

At last! at last! the wished-for moment came. The sun after reddening for a few minutes, sank behind the western horizon and I had preserved the honor of the Creek warrior and that of myself. I had not saved our troops from surprise or attack, but I certainly had obeyed the orders of my commanding general and stood watch as instructed until *sun down* and was now free to leave and seek to join our forces wherever they may be.

I took the track beaten out through the high weeds and grass by our retiring forces, which was visible enough except in the darkness of the deep bottoms where it was sometimes with difficulty that I could keep in the road. My present recollection is that I never reached our troops until the gray dawn of day was breaking. I made my report that the site of our late camps was duly provided with a watch as instructed and that at *sun down* no enemy had made his appearance. I think my remaining alone as watchman on this occasion was known but to the immediate members of my company only, and I am sure that the incident proved to my men the utter mistake and injustice

[16]The quotation is also from Thomas Gray's "Elegy Written in a Country Churchyard." *The Oxford Dictionary of Quotations,* 229 (28).

done me by those who were disposed to impute my former slowness to enlist in the army to lack of courage in case of danger. If this did not fully dispose of the imputation, other subsequent acts of mine I am confident did, as shall appear later.

CHAPTER SIX

Battling the Enemy

SOMETIME AFTER THIS a raid was planned to cross the enemy's line and attack a party of hay-makers who were encamped on the prairie north of the Verdagris [Verdigris] river under protection of a detachment of soldiers from Ft. Gibson. In this case the entire number of men volunteering to engage in the raid did not I think exceed three hundred. Major Howland of one of the Cherokee regiments was placed in command and in this number of raiders there were Cherokees and Creeks from both of the Creek regiments. I was of the number with a few men from my immediate company. I remember that my cousin Valentine N. McAnally elsewhere mentioned as being a month older than myself, who was a member of my company, was with me on this occasion.[1]

Crossing the Arkansas and Verdagris rivers after two days' march, we entered the fertile prairie on which the haying party and escort were encamped and operating. [We] did some long

[1] Stationed at Fort Gibson, the Union army haying party was apparently at work at a point between present-day Wagoner and Okay, Oklahoma. If Grayson remembered the sequence of events correctly, the action probably occurred sometime in early July, 1864, although it cannot be identified precisely in the *Official Records*. It certainly was not the Blackburn Prairie encounter of July 28 in the Cherokee Nation generally mentioned by historians. In engagements just west of Fort Smith on July 29, 1864, Gen. Douglas Cooper cited Maj. E. J. Howland for outstanding service and bravery. Howland found and guided back to safety a unit that had been separated from the main Confederate force. See Rampp and Rampp, *Civil War in the Indian Territory*, 96.

range firing at them with small arms and captured the camps of the hay makers. [After] burning the immense ricks of cured hay and whatever else we found combustible belonging to the enemy, we retired across the Verdagris. In this unimportant engagement one of our men, a mulatto named July, very foolishly charged upon a supposed empty log cabin and was shot and killed by an enemy from the inside, while an Indian (Creek) of the 2d Creek regiment named Ko-ne-a-ka was wounded in the hand. These were not, however, to be the sum of our casualties as subsequent events proved.

The raid so far was regarded by the men as eminently successful although at the cost of one life and a painful wound. The men had captured and appropriated many and various articles of value from the camps of the enemy when they charged them. Now as they were on their return they crossed the Verdagris and being tired and anxious to examine and see more closely the booty they had each taken, they halted on the south banks of the river where the bluffs were high and steep. Here the men dismounted; some going out of the bluffs turned their horses loose to drag the bridle reins and pick and eat the grass of the prairie which abutted directly up to the bluffs. Others remained down under the bluffs by the waters of the river, where those who had them munched hard tacks and drank river water.

The boys were much pleased, many of them, with their hauls, and were busily engaged in showing each other their goods, and trading, swapping and buying from one another in high glee. Having captured nothing myself, I was taking very little interest in the commerce so suddenly springing up on and under the banks of the Verdagris. Going up out of the bluffs on the top, I dismounted and, with my bridle reins in my hands, followed my horse around while he was picking the grass, which was very good here, awaited orders to march. Before such order was given, however, and while the trade was brisk upon and below the bluffs, the enemy whom we had ransacked and dispersed, having rallied, got together in considerable force, crept up through the bottoms on the opposite side and dealt us a volley from the thick brush, the stream being only about fifty yards wide here, which created a panic in our trade and dire consternation among the traders.

Men who had dropped their bridle reins giving their horses full liberty to graze on the grass at will were now running to and fro, calling to others to catch their horses for them. The horses when approached by frightened men would in turn become frighted at the unusual actions of their masters and scamper away, which but for its seriousness would have been in the highest degree laughable. Firing from the brush continued but only for a few moments. Even could our men have collected their terribly scattered wits, they could not have returned the fire of the enemy who was no where to be seen, being concealed by the great trees and brush on their side of the river. The men having succeeded in mounting their horses, stampeded out on the prairie some hundreds of yards away from where the attack was made on us and halted.

[We then] discovered that our commanding officer Major Howland was not with us. There were those who declared that that officer was wounded by the enemy's first volley. Capt. Sam Gunter of the Cherokees would probably be the next in command, and indeed was already rallying the men and apparently trying to get them into some shape for resistance or attack of the enemy. A few [of the latter] had now come over on our side of the river and were on the ground where only a few minutes ago we trafficked and traded in stuff we had taken from them. It seemed a shame to leave our wounded commander behind without making some effort toward finding what had been his fate; whether he had been overtaken by the enemy and despatched, or escaped and was in hiding in the thickets nearby whence we might rescue and carry him with us. A few of the enemy were in plain view riding about over the ground at the river.

What to do was the question that was uppermost with us. We held a council of war as it may be called, on horseback, when Capt. Gunter declared that if he could get a sufficient number of men to follow him, he would attack the enemy. Our men exhibited no mind for engaging in his proposed enterprise. I told the Captain that for one I would follow him. Bean

Burgess said he would also go; and while there may have been others who proffered their services, I do not now recall any. While we were yet talking, Capt. Gunter decided that he would not make the venture as he said he was himself wounded and in no proper condition for leading a fight. The captain, however, could hardly have been called wounded, as what he designated as a *wound* as I now recall was only this: one of the enemy's bullets had struck the large brass army buckle or clasp that fastened his leather belt in front, and without going through it had reddened and bruised the skin, and probably jarred him considerably at the moment of impact. This was all.[2]

[Yet] with this decision we, as I must say, ignominiously left the field and our commander without any effort toward determining his fate or rendering him any assistance. A detachment was sent out in two days afterward who found him making his way back to camps over the route traveled by his command, and brought him safely to camps.[3]

It seeming to be the policy of the military authorities to use our Indian brigade not so much for service outside of the Indian Territory as a menace to the enemy's southern line, we were constantly watching for weak places or insufficiently protected interests where we might run in, deliver a damaging blow and fly quickly to the cover of our base, which in the later years of the war was in the Choctaw nation. It was a kind of warfare that was suited to the Indian character, and in carrying out the policy we continually attracted the notice of the

[2]The Gunter family was prominent in Cherokee tribal affairs both before and after removal. The image of Samuel Gunter presented here by Grayson contrasts with that in official reports from General Cooper. In action late in July, 1864, near Fort Smith, Gunter cannonaded federal positions and with two others heroically swam the Arkansas River to capture Union couriers, and then swam back. See Cooper, In the field, to Capt. T. M. Scott, Aug. 10, 1864, *Official Records,* ser. i, vol. 41, pt. 1, 32–33. Although there were a number of Creeks with the same family name, Bean Burgess may have been a Cherokee. See *Campbell's Abstract of Creek Indian Census Cards and Index,* entry 2037, p. 133.

[3]"Camps" for the Confederate forces was so-called Camp Pike, located east of the Canadian River in the Choctaw Nation and one mile northwest of present-day Whitefield in Haskell County. See Marvin J. Hancock, "The Second Battle of Cabin Creek, 1864," *Chronicles of Oklahoma* 34 (Winter, 1961–62): 417n.

enemy to ourselves, thus keeping him from concentrating with others of his forces and aiding in giving effective battle to some of our larger armies which had already all of the enemy that they cared to deal with.

In aid of this policy Gen. Watie undertook to take in another haying camp on the north side of the Arkansas river in the Cherokee Nation not very distant from Ft. Smith.[4] He took personal command; and at a time when the river was high crossed it by the men swimming their horses and transporting their arms, ammunition and other necessaries across on rude rafts of cotton wood logs lashed together with ropes. I remember in the crossing a soldier belonging to Co. "A," 2d Creek regiment, was drowned. Having gotten over without further mishap, we marched very quietly until dark, and during much of the night. [Still we] had to stop and wait for hours, it being the scheme to come upon the enemy just at day light and surprise and take him in.

We got to their camps in the right time as planned. The general taking charge of the centre despatched his men composing his left to hasten around and take a certain position and bring on the attack. Capt. Young Hardridge of the 1st Creek regiment made the attack, and, the dully gray of dawn being not yet fully dispelled, the pyrotechnic effects of our attack, I remember, presented a grand scene. The enemy did not hold out long but began giving way before our fire, when our Seminole contingent made a rush to deliver an attack in the right where no fighting had yet been done. They had to go some several rods to accomplish this, and while going in double quick time, they set up a terrible yell and whoop that resounded all over the neighborhood.

Now it appeared that the Choctaws, none of whom were

[4]This haying camp of the federal army was located at Gunter's Prairie, just north of Fort Smith, Arkansas, in what is now eastern Sequoyah County, Oklahoma. Stand Watie and 500 men attacked units of the Second and Fourteenth Kansas Cavalry Regiments there on Aug. 24, 1864, killing 20 federals, capturing 14 prisoners, taking 150 horses, and burning a quantity of hay. See Franks, *Stand Watie*, 168–69, and Gen. Samuel Bell Maxey, Ft. Towson, to Col. S. S. Anderson, Sept. 3, 1864, *Official Records*, ser. i, vol. 41, pt. 1, 279; Rampp and Rampp, *Civil War in the Indian Territory*, 99.

with us on this raid, had the reputation with the enemy of being heartless and of never sparing the life of any enemy coming into their power. This was untrue but nevertheless confidently believed by the enemy. When our Seminoles made the hideous yells and charged the enemy's left they were mistaken for the deadly Choctaw; for, as the enemy thought, who but he could utter such blood-curdling noises. They reasoned that to yield their position and trust to flight for safety would mean their certain capture and massacre on the prairies adjoining their camps by these notorious and blood thirsty Choctaws, the only alternative being that of remaining where they were and fight it out. The latter alternative they adopted and those who were giving way preparatory to flight returned, and put up such a stiff resistance that we were after a while forced to reconsider our plans and give up the fight. Fearing a force from Ft. Smith might come up to give protection to this camp of haymakers and finding us cut off from our main body in the Choctaw Nation give us serious trouble, we hastened back and crossed the yet booming Arkansas over to our own side.

A short time after this, I think it was, a new commander came into our wing of the theatre of war and did some very creditable work. This was a Gen. [Richard M.] Gano who before being long in this department received information of a valuable train of wagons belonging to the enemy and all loaded with supplies for the post of Ft. Gibson, which was moving down from Ft. Scott, Kansas. He determined to go after and meet these people and if possible take them in. To do this, it required him to go some fifty or sixty miles north of Ft. Gibson, a pretty well garrisoned and otherwise equipped headquarters of the enemy, which had been used as such headquarters since shortly after the breaking out of hostilities.[5]

After several days of preparation, some two thousand men,

[5]Gen. Richard M. Gano commanded the Fifth Texas Cavalry Brigade, C.S.A. Born in Bourbon County, Kentucky, in June, 1830, he graduated from the Louisville Medical School and then practiced medicine until 1859, when he moved to Tarrant County, Texas. There he was elected to the state legislature and began a career as a minister of the Christian Church (or Church of Christ), holding the

as I believe, consisting of Creeks, Seminoles, Cherokees and Texans with a battery of four pieces of artillery were gotten in readiness for the expedition.[6] I joined this expedition, it having become my rule and purpose to take part in all proposed raids against the enemy when I had a horse in condition to withstand the hardships incident to such expeditions. It is perhaps right to explain here that such inclinations did not necessarily signify bravery, courage or desire in me for recklessly courting and facing danger as I found some of my associates interpreted it, but rather the dominating influence of the somewhat commonplace thirst for excitement and desire for action characteristic more or less of all young people.

We crossed the Canadian, the Arkansas and the Verdagris rivers after two days march and reached an encampment of negro hay makers about two miles beyond the present town of Wagoner, who were cutting and putting up hay for the use of the army at Ft. Gibson. There appeared to have been a small escort of negro soldiers, as nearly all the dead and prisoners were negroes, who for a few minutes after our attack returned our fire. One or two cannon shots of grape from our guns, however, caused a stampede, when we charged the encampment. The defenders disappeared among the thickets and very high weeds that covered the banks of the creek and for a few minutes after reaching the deserted camps it did not appear that there was anything for us to do more than burning the

---

same religious views as Robert Graham and William Baxter at Arkansas College. In the Civil War he first saw action in Kentucky, but transferred to the trans-Mississippi theater in 1863. After the war he devoted himself to his ministry in the Church of Christ until his death at Dallas, Texas, in March, 1913. During his lifetime he baptized some 7,000 persons. See Rampp and Rampp, *Civil War in the Indian Territory,* 155, and Stephen Daniel Eckstein, Jr., *History of the Churches of Christ in Texas, 1824–1950,* 180.

[6] The Indian Brigade numbered about 800 men. The Second Creek Regiment, of which Grayson was a part, included 200 men and was commanded on this expedition by Col. Timothy Barnett; Lt. Col. Samuel Checote led the 125 men of the First Creek Regiment. The Texas units numbered approximately 1,200 men. The combined force left Camp Pike on Sept. 14, 1864. See Hancock, "The Second Battle of Cabin Creek," 417–21, and Stand Watie, Camp Bragg, to T. B. Heiston, Oct. 3, 1864, *Official Records,* ser. i, vol. 51, pt. 1, 785.

camps and the great ricks of hay that stood about on the field.[7]

Presently, however, some of our men discovered a negro hiding in the high weeds near the creek and shot and killed him. At another point another one was found and shot, and it now appearing that these were to be found hid in the weeds, the men proceeded to hunt them out much as sportsmen do quails. Some of the negroes finding they were about to be discovered, would spring up from the brush and cry out, O! master spare me. But the men were in no spirit to spare the wretched unfortunates and shot them down without mercy. Some of them [Grayson's men] on other parts of the field had captured some six or eight, but where I was no negro was captured. Some of them were found lying in hiding in the creek with barely their noses out of the water and were shot and dragged and thrown out on the bank.

I confess this was sickening to me, but the men were like wild beasts and I was powerless to stop them from this unnecessary butchery. Toward the last one of our men found a young white man and brought him to where I sat on my horse and asked me, "Should we not kill him too?" or words to that effect. I told him not to kill him but to take and turn him in with the bunch of prisoners already taken, that it was negroes that we were killing now and not white men. Here was found some mother's son whom the fortunes of war had caught on the adverse side. Probably a good young man in the main, whose life hung for a moment upon a word from me while he was too frightened to talk or plead for his life. I sided with him and prolonged his life. My cousin Valentine N. McAnally was with this expedition and captured at this fight a chestnut sorrel mare from the enemy and rode her I think the rest of this raid.

[7]Occurring on Sept. 16, 1864, this battle took place near the mouth of Flat Rock Creek. The Union officer, Capt. E. A. Barker, commanded some 125 men, including a small unit of the Second Kansas Cavalry and a detachment of the First Kansas Colored Infantry. The Union forces suffered 100 casualties and the loss of all their equipment, haying machines, and approximately 3,000 tons of hay. See sources cited in n. 6 above, and Rampp and Rampp, *Civil War in the Indian Territory*, 104–106; and Britton, *Union Indian Brigade*, 437–40.

Our soldiers were poorly clad and most of the time my company presented a motley appearance. The Confederacy being hard run had very little in the way of clothing to issue to the men of this part of the country, and we were never very presentable. So when we caught a prisoner from the other side, we generally stripped him clean of such of his wearing apparel as we desired, they being always better than our own, and placed upon him instead such of our own old duds as he could wear. Our government had issued to our men certain wool hats which appeared to be manufactured of the plain sheep's wool without any coloring, while the hatter seemed not to have seriously concerned himself about the symmetry and poise of any individual hat. They were all apparently on one block and driven together in long stacks, and when one came near a stack of them he could distinctly discern the odor of the raw material. It smelled very like getting inside of a pen where a drove of sheep is confined. Now these hats, while not comely of shape and general appearance, had the further disadvantage of losing after a short service even the little shape and semblance of figure that had been given them by the manufacturers. The entire brim would invariably flop down, leaving little other signs of its former self than a dirty cotton string, while the crown, without any apparent provocation, would push sharply up in the centre, converting the whole into the exact figure of a cone. These hats being a dull whitish color were very susceptible to the effects of dust and dirt, and naturally had a dingy appearance at best, which became execrable after a month's wear.

One such hat that had well nigh served its time and collected its full share of dust and discolorations was owned and worn by McAnally. Being a young man of decidedly Indian taste in matters of dress and ornamentation, [he] embellished it in true aboriginal style with one of the plumes of the wing of the falcon, commonly known in the country as the chicken hawk, the shaft of which had been carefully pared away and rendered so thin, pliant and limber that the least air disturbance gave it to a vibratory or rather tremulous motion highly re-

Pleasant Porter as a Confederate Cavalryman, circa 1863. Later Porter served as principal chief of the Creeks from 1899 to 1907. He is dressed here in attire identical to that Grayson wore on his Civil War campaigns. *Smithsonian Institution, National Anthropological Archives.*

sponsive to the Indian's idea of esthetics. This feather he had securely fastened in the apex of this hat where it had for considerable time done service doubtless to the admiration of his comrades in war.

Having through his own courage and proclivities for warlike deeds captured a little old, tall, lank and woebegone appearing fellow of the enemy, Mack proceeded to relieve him of such of his clothing as he desired which would fit him. He took also his hat which he considerately replaced with this own typical Confederate hat, feather ornament and all, and when a moment later I met him in another part of the field, I could hardly recognize him as the same, he being now so differently decked out from what he was when he first met the enemy. He explained how he had captured a prisoner with whom he had made some exchanges of clothing, and how he believed he could point him out to me among the number of those that had been taken.

At a certain point the prisoners taken in the afternoon's work were filing by when he pointed out the unfortunate who was the unwilling cause of his being a hero. He was the most miserable, forlorn and wretched appearing and gangling little, old white man anywhere in sight. On his Confederate hat's apex was blithely and bravely trembling to the breeze his Ke-ak-ka-ta-fa (falcon's feather), while he with down cast countenance marched slowly along in evident ignorance of the gaity and life supposed to be typified by the plumed head gear he wore. Of all the supremely ludicrous, ridiculous, laughable objects I had ever been up against this was the crowning one. I enjoyed a big laugh at McAnally's prisoner.

From here we moved on after bigger game.[8] In two days thereafter, as I now recall, we reached the encampment of the

---

[8] From prisoners taken at Flat Rock, Watie and Gano learned that the large Union supply train they hoped to find was expected daily at Fort Gibson from Fort Scott, Kansas. Indeed, a train of 205 government wagons and 91 sutler wagons with armed teamsters had left the Kansas post on Sept. 12, 1864, escorted by 260 men of the Second, Sixth, and Fourteenth Kansas Cavalry who were commanded by Maj. Henry Hopkins. Following the Texas Road, the train reached the crossing at Cabin Creek on Sept. 18, 1864, where it was met by 310 Union Cherokees of the Second and Third Indian (Home Guard) Regiments as well as other volunteer forces. The settlement at the crossing, situated in what is now Craig County south of Vinita, included private residences, a stage station, and a military stockade, the latter established in 1863 and offering some protection for the train. Only hours after the 300 plus wagons arrived at Cabin Creek, General Gano's Confederate scouts discovered their location. The ensuing battle

enemy early in the morning, the fires of which we could clearly see for quite a considerable distance before we were sufficiently near to offer them battle. Arriving, however, in easy reach and it being yet dark, we formed in order of battle and stood, awaiting the light of day when we could see how to meet in dispute the men of which we had come so far to see.

While we were quietly awaiting the light, it appeared quite clear from the boisterous and careless talk of the enemy, which we could plainly hear, that there had been some drinking, and that at least some of the men were now under the influence of drink. Some of them called at us, "What are you doing here? What do you want?" Some of our men answered, "We are after you and your mule teams and wagons." Presently one of the enemy who evidently was drunk, after heaping upon us all manner of vile epithets and curses, started over our way, never ceasing his curses as he came. He came as I recall in such way as to reach the south end of our line as we stood, and presently one of our men called to him, Halt! He appeared to pay no heed to the challenge but continued his imprecations and his advance when we again heard the call to, halt! This did not check his movement so the third and last challenge was made and within a few moments a shot, then another and all was quiet.

After some minutes more of waiting, when it began to be light enough to see what we had come against we observed some two or three houses in a stockaded inclosure which was garrisoned with soldiers, but what their numbers were we could not know. A large number of wagons, with the teams of mules that drew them standing by, [were] in a circle around the grounds [with] armed men . . . about them—guards perhaps. There now began occasional desultory firing from the enemy and from our own men although our orders were not to fire until orders for attack was given. A single shot from the enemy I distinctly recall sped a bullet that struck the ground

on the bluffs of the south bank of the river began about 3:00 A.M. in full moonlight and lasted until 9:00 A.M., Sept. 19, 1864. See Rampp and Rampp, *Civil War in the Indian Territory,* 108–16; and Britton, *Union Indian Brigade,* 441–46.

very near and in front of our lines and near to where I stood
with my company. Notwithstanding my orders were not to fire
until I so ordered, a member of my company known as "Captain Dorsey" (although a private) could not stand to be so bul-
lied, and fired his trusty musket in the direction of the enemy.
I reprimanded Dorsey for his disobedience of orders, when he
replied that he had not come all the way here to stand quietly
by while the enemy deliberately shot at him.

It was now light enough for us to see what we should do,
and the order coming to us to *fire,* our men obeyed with alac-
rity and spirit, and things certainly began now to appear decidedly warlike.[9] I stood in front of my men talking to them in
terms of encouragement, and the flash and smoke of their guns
would at some moments quite cover me and sometimes hide
me from view. Seeing this, McAnally as soon as he had a fair
opportunity came and quietly warned me that our men were
fighting under much excitement and some were liable to shoot
me accidentally, and that instead of moving about in front of
them I had best either fall into ranks or immediately back of
the men. I remembered, however, that somebody had in the
earlier history of our enlistment intimated that I was tardy
about enlisting because of the fear of danger. This was always
an unpleasant remembrance, and it had always been my desire
to prove to the contrary in open court, and here was some real
fighting where I might exhibit my true self in the presence of
my detractors and where there was real danger, and I was determined to improve the opportunity come what may.

I had one man wounded—Its-hoh-he, otherwise Nu-cus
E-mah-thlu-tse by name, of the Okfuskeys—who was led back
to the rear to be cared for while the exciting work of endeavoring to overpower the enemy and capture his property went
bravely on. Our artillery was brought to bear upon him and
was continually belching forth its death-dispensing contents
toward his vitals, but was obstinate and refused to acknowl-

---

[9] Grayson's unit was stationed on the extreme left flank of the Confederate line
with other Indian troops; the Texans were in the middle and on the right flank.
Watie, Camp Bragg, to Heiston, Oct. 3, 1864, *Official Records,* ser. i, vol. 51,
pt. 1, 785.

edge the force of the argument we were putting up. The early morning atmosphere was decidedly cool and light and soon became so charged with the heavier smoke of battle as to completely obstruct all view of the enemy, in consequence of which a cessation of hostilities for a few minutes was ordered.

Before resuming, and while waiting in line for further orders, some members of my company having great faith in certain Indian war medicine said to afford protection against the casualties of battle, produced the medicine, talisman or whatever the article was (I never saw it) and distributed it to those who desired its protection, which they proceeded to use by rubbing it on and about the clothing of the body and limbs as thoroughly as they could within the limited time they had for taking the treatment. My first lieutenant Tsup-ofe Fix-ico—Thomas Benton as he was called in English—I distinctly recall, offered to supply me with a treatment saying, "Aren't you going to use this?" I declined his proffered kindness, it still being in me to prove to these men that I was willing to risk myself in the presence of danger under the impulses of my innate courage without resorting to the supposed protection afforded by medicines or talismans, and prove to them that I could meet risks as coolly as the bravest soldier under me, and was not the man to shirk danger as some at one time seemed to think I was.

We were ordered to dismount, and being afoot now we resumed firing on the enemy and moved up on him. While we were down on one knee and foot and making things as hot as possible for him, one of my men, of the Eufaula town, named "Lawyer," who had for some reason lagged behind, moved up to where I was pumping bullets at the enemy, and in Indian asked, "Where are they?" "There they are," I said, pointing in the direction of the enemy, "give them fits if you can." In ready obedience he proceeded to deliver the attack of epilepsy as ordered, by discharging a long flint lock squirrel rifle with which he was armed at the enemy, holding it in his excitement only a few inches away from the left side of my face. The particles of shattered flint from his flint lock and all the priming of the touch-pan, at the discharge flew into my face break-

ing the skin near the left eye and causing some show of blood,
and for the nonce completely blinded me. This was no proper
place for a blind man and I fell to busily rubbing and trying to
restore the power of seeing to my now crippled visual organ,
in which I soon succeeded. The burnt powder from Lawyer's
gun that blew into the broken skin created a tiny blue spot in
the cuticle near the left eye which has never disappeared, and
I suppose never will.

I had loudly encouraged and cheered my men from the first,
speaking always in Indian, until my voice gave way under the
continued strain, and was now only a whisper and could
scarcely be heard at all. The wing of the firing line on which I
was stationed was now re-enforced by a detachment of Texans,
and shortly the fighting seemed to wax hotter than at any other
time causing me to realize the very striking fact that a large
number of bullets were not striking me. We had advanced and
fell back several times, and, as elsewhere indicated, my men
having never been either drilled or subjected to regular army
discipline, we became mixed up with our Texan comrades and
others. Many individual members were fighting and conducting themselves as seemed to them best, when a charge was
ordered. I remember joining the Texans in the charge and going on without interruption up to and within the protecting
stockades.

Pleasant Porter always told me afterwards that, being with
the charge when the stockades were taken, he looked about
him and saw not a single Creek besides himself when there
had been so many on the firing line in the battle proper. [He]
was just experiencing a feeling of regret that the Creeks did
not have a greater representation in this crowning act of actual
victory, when looking over a few steps from where he stood,
he saw me, the only other Creek, and felt an experience of
relief. [It was] a sort of feeling as if the honor of the Creeks in
this engagement in which we were victorious had been sufficiently vindicated.

The enemy took to their heels and the brush near by, leaving
everything while our men engaged in the capturing and appro-
priating such portable articles of value, horses, mules, guns,

and trunks of goods and whatever else came handy. I gathered and carried away a large valise I found in one of the houses in the stockades, but which on examination I found to contain nothing of any considerable value. The wagons, about 150 in number and all loaded with valuable merchandise, [and] mule teams to draw them, in the finest condition now after so much fighting, stood in considerable confusion. But drivers were soon detailed to the task of conducting them safely "away down south in Dixie," and without losing any time we headed this valuable property, with the boys in gray this time as escort, for our own headquarters, which now, since we had departed on this expedition, had been moved to the north of the Canadian river.[10]

We did not move but a short distance from the field of battle on our return, before we were met by a small force, presumably from Ft. Gibson, with some artillery, which took a number of shots at us, but without effect. We might have taken this force in, but had now so much of value to care for, and being so far within the enemy's lines, we deemed the safe plan the better and simply described a detour to the right under shelter of certain high grounds and came on without further molestation, crossing the Arkansas river at the point where the town of Tulsa is now located.[11] For a long time afterwards this ford on the river was known as *Gano's crossing*.

From this crossing we continued our forced march toward home, stopping in a regular camp over night for the first time since undertaking the expedition somewhere not distant from the town of Okmulkee [Okmulgee]. At this time there was no such town. From here we moved south over to the Canadian river where our reserves were encamped, and where we stopped

[10] Southern sources set the value of the Union train at $1,500,000. As the battle had damaged many of the supplies and other items, the Confederates could salvage only 740 mules and 130 wagons filled with much-needed booty. In the battle itself only 20 Union and 9 Confederate soldiers were killed. See Franks, *Stand Watie*, 172.

[11] With their captured stores and wagons, the Confederates had first started south, but were met at Pryor's Creek by units of the 79th U.S. Colored Troops commanded by Col. J. M. Williams. They then turned southwest, crossing the Verdigris River near Claremore Mounds and the Arkansas at Tulsa. Hancock, "The Second Battle of Cabin Creek," 420.

for a good rest, and where the stuff captured was distributed to the captors and others. This was certainly the most trying expedition I have ever been engaged in, as we never unsaddled our horses since crossing the Arkansas river in the going until we again crossed it on the return and camped as stated near Okmulkee, covering a period of some five or six days. I sometimes would sleep while in the saddle, riding along for miles, and cannot yet understand how it happened that I did not fall from my horse.

While resting up at Camp Canadian many were the yarns that were spun by the men of the expedition around our campfires.[12] While there seemed to be nothing occurring in the recent engagement through which we had successfully passed that was of a diverting character, it was remarkable how many laughable stories the men had to tell of themselves and others, as incidents of the fight. A certain little old Indian, Yul-ke Ha-tsu by name, during the engagement annoyed me not a little by trying to show himself off a great hero, or fighting man. He broke ranks and would go for perhaps a rod in advance of our line calling to the men, "If you be the men you in time of peace and security claim to be, come out from the lines and do as I do." Concluding his harangue he would fire in the air toward the enemy his own dragoon pistol commonly called a "horse pistol," and wheeling back to our lines taunt his friends with their lack of bravery. This he did a number of times against my orders not to break ranks and much to my annoyance. When we made the last and successful charge on the enemy's stockades, a mule lay dead near by that had been completely disemboweled by a shot from our artillery, which was quite a conspicuous object to those engaged in that part of the field. One member of our company, Etsu Ema thala, relating to a comrade this circumstance, told how great a hero Yul-ke Ha-tsu tried to think himself to be on the field of battle; and how despite the orders to reserve his fire for a better opportunity, he persisted in fighting our battles almost singly and alone with his *horse pistol,* shooting high up in the air toward

[12] In official reports "Camp Canadian" was identified by Stand Watie as "Camp Bragg."

the enemy. He related that when we charged and reached the enemy's stronghold and looked about us, what should we see but a fine large mule lying dead on the ground with its entrails and life blood flashed about for some distance around it, the gory and sickening evidences of the terrible effectiveness of Yul-ke Ha-tsu's unerring aim with his trusty equine pistol.

One evening when the men had been for some hours reeling off to each other yarns funny and otherwise and conversation was lagging I recall distinctly how Jackson Mun-ah-we arose from where he had been sitting. Starting to go to the fire to light his pipe, [he] remarked, "When under our former captain we made loud complaints of his lack of courage to lead us to battle. We charged that he was cowardly. I am sure we have nothing to complain of now." The former captain was an old man and really not a man for action, and least of all, military action; but was put in the office because he was old and re-garded as one of the wise men of the Eufaula town of Indians. Much had been said in complaint against his inactivity, and this remark of Mun-ah-we was meant for a compliment to me, and was so understood by all.[13] I never for a moment expected such a compliment, as Indians rarely ever say things compli-mentary to a person in his presence. This was therefore all the more gratifying to me, as proving that I had fully succeeded in satisfying my friends, and my enemies if I had any, that I could, and would willingly go as far toward meeting a danger-ous proposition as any other of my age and experience. I knew now that I had fully cleared away all possible grounds for any one to think that I lacked the courage to face danger in battle as had at one time been intimated, and I was highly pleased.

I, however, have sometimes doubted whether I was entitled to any credit for what others regarded as courage in me for the reasons that at that time I was but a boy and probably did not fully appreciate the dangers around me. I don't think I did. The brave and courageous man, in my present more mature judg-

---

[13] Although the record is not certain, Jackson Mun-ah-we was, if not the son, then related to the famous Red Stick leader who had survived the battle of Horse-shoe Bend to be the principal executioner of William McIntosh in 1825. See Chap. 1, n. 14.

ment, is he who in his normal mental condition clearly sees as he believes imminent danger and even probable death before him, and yet without shrinking, coldly faces and goes into it, because, as he believes, it is his duty to do so. Again I believe there are those who are borne along on the wave of personal pride, who are impelled to action and incidental exhibition of personal courage by the idea that whatever men have done or are doing, another may do.

Pleasant Porter, who was afterward prominent in our public affairs and finally became chief of the nation, and I served near together in the army much of the time during the last years of the war, he being 1st lieutenant in Co. A of the same regiment I served in.[14] He on one occasion told me that when going into battle it was always his custom to commend himself to the help and protection of God. This I never did and, I suspect, was guilty of the shortcoming once attributed by Robert Jones to the Choctaws.[15] Uncle Watt Grayson was in conversation with Jones, himself a Choctaw, and drifting from one to other topics introduced that of the well known bravery of the full blood Choctaw in battle, and asked him why they were so fearless and brave. Jones answered that it was simply because *they had no sense.* I fear that like the full blood Choctaw I did not have sense enough to be other than what I was. I have therefore to thank my good fortune for having weathered the storm and [that I] am even yet able to write these memoirs.

[14] Stand Watie singled out Lt. Pleasant Porter for special praise in the capture of seven Union soldiers at the battle of Flat Rock Creek. See Watie to Heiston, Oct. 3, 1864, *Official Records,* ser. i, vol. 51, pt. 1, 785.

[15] Robert M. Jones was a wealthy Choctaw slaveholder, planter, and merchant who also exercised a leadership role in tribal politics. He was especially active in persuading the Choctaws to join the Confederacy and later served as tribal delegate to the Confederate Congress. See T. Paul Wilson, "Delegates of the Five Civilized Tribes in the Confederate Congress," *Chronicles of Oklahoma* 53 (Fall, 1975): 362–63.

CHAPTER SEVEN

The Shadow of Death

HOW LONG AFTER this [the Cabin Creek expedition] it was I do not know, but we were encamped on and about the lands now composing Mrs. Grayson's and Washie's lands allotted to them by the Dawes Commission in the general distribution of Creek lands.[1] Sometime in the month of December . . . Major James McHenry of the 1st Creek regiment organized an expedition to go and engage a squad of the enemy who it was reported were occupying the now abandoned village of the U.S. Creek Agency 3 or 4 miles northwest from the present town of Muscogee [Muskogee] whence scouts were being sent out south from time to time.[2] Following my penchant for raids and excitement, I joined the expedition.

[1] Grayson was apparently encamped in and around present-day Eufaula for more than a month. Throughout Oct. and Nov., 1864, Stand Watie's First Indian Brigade, to which Grayson's regiment was attached, operated in the area of North Fork Town and east toward Fort Smith, Arkansas. The unit's headquarters, however, remained at Camp Bragg on the Canadian. Just after the raid here described as occurring in Dec., 1864, Watie went into winter quarters at Boggy Depot, Choctaw Nation. See Franks, *Stand Watie,* 174–176. "Mrs. Grayson" was the autobiographer's wife, Anna Stidham, and "Washie" was his son Wash. The Dawes Commission was the government agency assigned the responsibility of enrolling the Five Tribes, allotting the common land individually, and terminating tribal government early in the twentieth century; the assigned lands here identified were located just south of the North Fork River, some three miles west and four miles north of Eufaula, where they are now inundated by the lake. See Creek Allotment Rolls, Records of the Dawes Commission, Manuscript Division, Oklahoma Historical Society.

[2] The son of a Scotch trader and an Indian mother, James McHenry had in

As the weather was ideal and the distance to our objective only about forty five miles, I did not provide sufficiently as afterwards appeared against eventualities of the season. When we were within ten or twelve miles of the Agency the skies became overcast with threatening clouds which emitted vivid lightning with deafening peals of thunder, and it soon was evident that the heavens with old Borcas in full control were against us, for now a cold wind met us from the north. I had started from camp without a coat of any kind, and as a provision against this sort of weather, I had only [a] small Mexican blanket which soon was wet through and through. We proceeded, however, until we reached the empty town and found none to dispute our entry. The wind and cold was increasing every moment in intensity, and it behooved us (especially me) to get away and back to camps as soon as possible.

Accordingly we set fire to all the principal unoccupied buildings as soon as possible. After warming ourselves for a little time by the great flames that shot up in the air from the burning buildings, we began a forced march for our camps on the North Fork river 45 miles away. As we started out of the little place, I distinctly recall coming up to the former home of Judge G. W. Stidham in the south edge of town, one of the best residences in the place, the home where Mrs. Grayson as a little twelve year old girl had lived and played but which had long been deserted, and ordering it set on fire and moving away while it still burned. I knew nothing of Mr. Stidham's daughter Anna who was to become to me the greatest woman in all the world.[3]

The most, indeed four fifths of our course lay over a bare

1836 led a rebellion against removal of the Creeks from Alabama, for which he was later captured and, in chains, was sent west. In Oklahoma he converted to Methodism, became a successful agriculturalist, and provided distinguished leadership for his people before and after the Civil War. The U.S. government agency and administrative offices, around which a small community of tradesmen and merchants had gathered, was situated four miles northwest of present-day Muskogee at Fern Mountain. It was located at that site in 1851 and remained there until 1874, when it was removed to the western edge of the town and became Union Agency. Debo, *Road to Disappearance,* 101, 121, 180.

[3] See Chap. 2, n. 5.

prairie, with nothing to break the force of the freezing winds. My blanket which had been thoroughly wet by the rain now froze, and in its frozen condition seemed to screen me from the blasts of north wind that were showing no mercy to man or beast better than it did before it froze, as the cold winds could not penetrate through the substance of the blanket and the ice that had formed in its interstices. I never in life before or since suffered from cold as I did on this occasion. At one time it was reported down the line that one of our men, an Indian, was likely to freeze and his friends had to stop to kindle a fire for his relief, but I never learned what truth there was in the report as I was myself too near frozen to sympathize with or try to help anyone. We reached the Col. D. N. McIntosh place on Pecan Creek at about sun set, and there dismounted, entered the house and with boards and fence rails built up great fires as quickly as possible and warmed ourselves.[4]

We remained about these fires until daylight, as I recollect, when we set out across the bare waste of prairies for the Deep Fork bottoms on the south. I as well as others rode in brisk gallop across this entire prairie of something like ten or more miles with the weather still fearfully cold. I can never forget how warm and pleasant it felt to me when I had passed through the terrible cold of that long prairie ride and struck the wooded bottoms of the Deep Fork.[5] Thus ended the last hostile raid as I recall that I ever engaged in against our common enemy.

[4]Born in Sept., 1822, Daniel N. McIntosh was a half brother of Chilly and a younger son of William McIntosh, the principal leader of the Lower Creeks prior to removal who was executed by Mun-ah-we and others for signing in 1825 the infamous Treaty of Indian Springs. D. N. attended Smith Institute in Tennessee, encouraged Creek affiliation with the Confederacy, and was colonel of the First Creek Regiment, participating in the battles of Round Mountain, Pea Ridge, and Honey Springs as well as other engagements. After the war he helped negotiate the Creek reconstruction treaty with the United States, contributed to the drafting of the new constitution of 1867, and served frequently as tribal delegate to Washington. His Pecan Creek residence was located some seven miles west of Muskogee. See D. C. Gideon, *Indian Territory,* 448; O'Beirne and O'Beirne, *Indian Territory* 1:379; and Meserve, "MacIntoshes," 321–22.

[5]A tributary to the North Fork, the Deep Fork of the Canadian cuts through northern McIntosh and southern Okmulgee counties, rising in Logan County just southeast of Guthrie.

After this our army gradually made its way back toward the Red river, the northern boundary of Texas.

One day when we were encamped at no considerable distance north of Boggy Depot in the Choctaw Nation, orders came for us to move camp and march on to Wah-pa-nah-ke [Wapanucka] Creek the next day.[6] I awoke the next morning with excruciating pain in my back which well nigh disabled me for any service or even for moving, but I saddled my horse and directing my men to move with the army and without me as I was too ill to keep up with the march, I leisurely and with much suffering from the pain in my back followed on horseback as best I could. Reaching Boggy Depot where I learned we had a hospital, I after considerable hunting found the institution and applied for admission. Asked what was the nature of my illness I assured them that from the symptoms I was experiencing, I believed I was being attacked by the Smallpox. The authorities very readily acquiesced in my diagnosis of my case and at once proceeded to inform me of their great sorrow because of the absence of any accommodations for me in the institution.

In great misery and some fever now I continued my ride in the wake of the army just preceding me. Arriving at the encampment on Wah-pa-nah-ke creek I found the particular camps of my own company, laid down and remained with them over night. It was advised that I be removed to a shelter, a house where I could be cared for more properly than it was possible to do in a camp without tents in the woods. By this time the fever was high on me and I do not now recall, if indeed I ever knew, how I got into a house. But there was a large stone school building within about a mile of our encampment, known in the neighborhood as Rock Academy, which in time of peace had been used in housing and schooling the children of the Chickasaw Nation but which now since the war was not being so used.[7]

[6] See Chap. 4, n. 10, and Chap. 5, n. 1.
[7] See Chap. 5, n. 1. Grayson's illness apparently occurred sometime in Feb., 1965.

Chickasaw Rock Academy, or Wapanucka, built in 1852. Grayson recovered here from smallpox during the Civil War. *Western History Collections, University of Oklahoma.*

My next recollection is when I found myself occupying a pallet on the floor of a northeast room of this building. My aunt Feenie elsewhere mentioned in these memoirs, whose husband Bradford Johnson was a Chickasaw, was, as were others, living with her son Robert Sewell at this house, and when I was brought there, she at once addressed herself to looking after my wants.[8] But there was really nothing to do more than to watch and keep the patient as comfortable as possible and let the illness take its course. While lying here the high fever that always accompanies a bad case of smallpox ran riot with me. For some time [it] had me as crazy as a loon, seeing possible and impossible things and trying on one occasion to shoot a number of Choctaws as I thought who had taken me prisoner. I do not think there has ever been a time when my reason was so completely dethroned as then.

By this time the news of my serious illness had reached

[8] For reference to Aunt Feenie, the younger sister of Grayson's mother, see Chap. 1.

Mother who with the rest of the children was living about forty miles still farther south on the Red river.[9] She immediately had two ponies saddled when she and brother Sam set out to find me. She was exceedingly anxious to find and see me once more alive but was very fearful that she was not going to have this pleasure. She and Sam arrived, however, one day and were informed that I still lived though very ill. I distinctly recall her coming into my sick room with what seemed a glad smile on her face, which she afterward told me was indeed a smile for she was overjoyed at seeing me alive even if I did die later.

[Mother] stayed in one end of the same room with me and watched and did for me whatever our regimental surgeons Drs. Colley and Hall prescribed until the pustules began to break out on me, which was very painful. My skin was literally a rotten mass from the top of my head to my toes, no part of my body escaping. My face was swollen and puffed up beyond recognition, my eyes closed so I could not see. The suppurations emitted an offensiveness that none perhaps but a fond mother actuated by her undying love for her boy could have borne. This was told me by Mother after I had recovered. When my clothing was being changed it was found to have stuck fast to my body and was not removed without excruciating pain to me. My hair which in accordance with the fashion at the time was very long, all came off of my head in cakes of tangled mass of corruption and putrescence. I would hardly have been recognized by any one who had known me a short time previous to the attack of this most loathsome disease.

Although our regimental physicians—two in number—were calling to see me at stated intervals they seemed powerless to

[9]Grayson never comments upon the circumstances of his family following their flight south after the battle of Honey Springs. Doubtless they joined other Creek refugees along Red River and its tributaries, suffering deprivations similar to those of the Cherokees best described by Angie Debo in "Southern Refugees of the Cherokee Nation," *Southwestern Historical Quarterly* 35 (April, 1932): 255–66. Later in this chapter Grayson places the family quarters in Pontotoc County, Chickasaw Nation, but "forty miles still farther south" of Wapanucka would put it in Panola County, the southeastern most of the four Chickasaw counties. See John W. Morris, Charles R. Goins, and Edwin C. McReynolds, *Historical Atlas of Oklahoma*, 2d ed., map 42.

render any service that in any appreciable way ameliorated my condition, save the administering of an occasional dose of morphine to alleviate the terrible pains caused by the mass of sores covering my body. At last one afternoon these doctors gave it out that I could not recover and would die at about four o'clock that evening. The news came to Mother from the outside and she communicated it to me. Now I felt that I was certainly sick enough to die, and I remember well that the information of the near approach of my dissolution occasioned me neither surprise or alarm. I felt confident that the change would relieve me of the terrible pain and misery now possessing me, and I cared little how soon it came. I knew of a grave yard nearby, having been at this school building before I was brought to it ill, and directed Mother to have my remains interred there, and remember distinctly thinking that at the resurrection at the last day spoken of in holy writ, I would see, as they arose out of their graves, what appearing people those were who were previously buried there although strangers to me.

Well, I did not die, and I have often regarded the fact that I did not as somewhat remarkable. Here I was sick enough to die, was told I would die soon, believed it and was in my own way of thinking, ready and willing, and yet death did not come. On the contrary I began to appear somewhat improved, and my recovery began from this very evening, and tho very slow, continued uninterruptedly until I was able to leave the place, having been confined to the sick room for an entire month.

Some one, probably brother Sam, brought horses from our home on Red river for each of us, and Mother and I bade adieu to the hospitable old roof and room that had held us so long in our dire affliction. The clouds gathered in the skies, however, before we had proceeded very far and a slow rain set in that continued the rest of the day and penetrated some portions of my clothing to the skin. We continued our course, however, until we reached the Seminole encampment on Glasses Creek late in the evening when nearly dark.[10] Riding up to the cabin

[10] Located south of the Washita River, Glasses Creek flows east and south

of a Seminole, Mother asked shelter and lodgings for the night. Being only refugees and lodged in hastily improvised cabins prepared for the accommodation of the immediate members of the family only, as were these Seminoles, none of them as we well knew was able without sacrifice of his own comfort to take in travelers. But this noble old Seminole, I remember, said, "This not being a boat that might capsize and precipitate us in the water, you may stay with us."

From here we continued our way, the next morning reaching our own cabin in Pontotoc County, Chickasaw Nation, in good hour. Mother had at least succeeded in reuniting all of her children alive.[11] It was a long time before I was able for duty of any kind. In the meantime I was such a shocking object in appearance, with hair all gone, eye brows and lashes all gone, pits all over my once smooth face, weight from one hundred and seventy down to about a hundred. All conspired to make me averse to being seen, especially since previous to all this I easily persuaded myself that I was possessed of an average degree of good looks which had now completely vanished.

Sometime previous to my attack, Pleasant Porter approached me and asked me to go with him out some distance in the country away from our camps to a dance. Upon his earnest insistence I somewhat reluctantly agreed and went with him and attended the function, which was pulled off at a little cabin about 12 × 12 feet in what seemed an isolated spot in the woods unoccupied now, but which it was said had some time previously been occupied by some one afflicted with the Smallpox. Porter hence always lay [laid?] the blame upon himself for my affliction with the disease that came so nearly relegating me to the bone yard.

---

of Madill in present-day Marshall County and is the major western tributary of Lake Texoma.

[11] See n. 9 above. As Pontotoc County was the most northern of the Chickasaw counties, Grayson's memory fails him here. The site of the family cabin would have been on the Red River in present-day Marshall County, and now probably it is beneath the waters of Lake Texoma.

CHAPTER EIGHT

Peace and Home

I REMAINED ABOUT my home endeavoring to get myself again in shape for service in the army, but flesh and strength came slowly. About when I thought I might in a feeble way be able to resume my place in the service, it was rumored that the war was over. From a rumor it in a short time came to be authoritatively reported that Gen. Lee had surrendered and hostilities between the north and the south had ceased. No one knew anything of the terms of the surrender or could offer any reasonable suggestion as to what its effects would be on the Indian tribes who had been engaged in abetting the cause of the Confederacy now down and out. Everybody was at a loss as to how to plan for the future.[1]

After many wild rumors among the people as to the future policy that should govern the course of these southern tribes, our men who had been our military leaders in the war just now closing received an invitation from special commissioners of the Federal government to meet with them at Fort Smith, Arkansas, for the purpose of discussing peace terms now that the war between the states wherein they had taken active part, had ceased. In response to this, an international meeting of repre-

---

[1]Gen. Robert E. Lee surrendered the Army of Northern Virginia to U.S. Grant on April 9, 1865, at Appomattox Court House, Virginia. Gen. Edmund Kirby-Smith surrendered the armies of the Confederacy's Trans-Mississippi Department on May 26, 1865, and Stand Watie surrendered troops under his command, including the Creek regiments, on June 25, 1865.

sentatives of all the tribes in interest was held in the main building of one of the Choctaw national schools known as Armstrong Academy. I attended for my personal information and not as a representative of any one or a tribe. I returned home while men, older heads than I, were appointed who went and met the commissioners and arranged a sort of protocol and *modus vivendi* that lasted until a more elaborate treaty was afterwards negotiated in Washington, D.C. The terms of this Fort Smith agreement enabled our people to begin consideration of plans for removal back to their own country from which they had been absent so long.[2]

Being now out of employment, and my health fully restored, I had time to devote to my own personal amusement and intermingled quite freely with the young people of the neighborhood attending Indian ball games, stomp dances and such like sports, and came to be very friendly with many of the Chickasaws whom I met. By far the most respectable and prominent family for many miles around was a family of Chickasaws named James. Mr. Booker James had a daughter, Molsie, some eighteen or nineteen years old living with her uncle in the near neighborhood. The people soon became busy planning a marital relationship between her and me and creating among themselves quite a decided agreement that it was a

[2] The Grand Council of the United Nations of Indian Territory (see Chap. 4, n. 1) had met with the Plains tribes at Camp Napoleon on the Washita River near present-day Verden on May 24, 1865, to plan cooperative strategy for a rapprochement with the federal government. Following the surrender of the Confederate Indian troops, tribal leaders scheduled another meeting of the council for Sept. 1, 1865, at Armstrong Academy, expecting to meet with government negotiators to work out final peace agreements. Located two miles north of present-day Bokchito in Bryan County, Armstrong Academy served as the capitol of the Choctaw Nation for 20 years. At the last minute federal officials altered plans and called the tribes to Fort Smith, Arkansas, to undertake negotiations beginning Sept. 8, 1865. As Grayson indicates, the leaders of the pro-southern Indians did meet at Armstrong on Sept. 1, but following some strategy sessions they adjourned to Fort Smith. Discussions there were inconclusive, creating the necessity of opening new negotiations in Washington, D.C., the following spring. D. N. McIntosh and James M. C. Smith represented the Southern Creeks, while Sands, Coweta Micco, and Cotchoche spoke for the Loyal Creeks. Concluded in June and proclaimed in August, the Treaty of 1866 reestablished relationships between the Creeks and the United States, but to the great disadvantage of the Indians. See Debo, *Road to Disappearance,* 164–76.

INDIAN TERRITORY, 1844-1865

CHEROKEE OUTLET

ARKANSAS RIVER

CIMARRON RIVER

NORTH FORK OF CANADIAN RIVER

CANADIAN

WASHITA RIVER

CHICKASAW

CREEK

VERDIGRIS

CHEROKEE

GRAND RIVER

2nd Cabin
Creek

Flat
Rock
Creek

TULSA

Tahlequah

Park
Hill

WAGONER

Fort
Gibson

Pecan
Creek

MUSKOGEE

Honey Springs

EUFAULA

North Fork Town

Briartown

Pleasant
Bluff

Sans Bois
Creek

Brazil
Creek

Skully-
ville

Gaines
Creek

Perryville

CHOCTAW

RIVER

KIAMICHI

Texas Road

Wapanucka

Boggy
Depot

Fort Washita

Glasses
Creek

Armstrong
Academy

RED

ISLAND BAYOU
RIVER

0 10 20 30 40 50

Creek stick ball game near Okemah, Oklahoma, circa 1910. *Western History Collections, University of Oklahoma Library.*

consummation much to be desired. More in acquiescence in this prevailing neighborhood opinion than my own inclinations, I paid court to Miss James and in a short time offered myself and was accepted.[3]

I had to aid in caring for Mother and the children, however, and could not think of just then taking on the care of a wife. [I] suggested that our nuptials be not celebrated until after I had visited my desolated old home and provided there for Mother and the children, which was quite satisfactory to her. I do not believe there was any such love in our engagement as should be between two persons entering so serious an agreement. Miss James was possessed of many cattle and other live stock and probably money; I had nothing; and when I came back to the old home and saw the general desolation, I was too proud to ask her to share my penury and poverty, and after a time wrote asking her to release me from my engagement, which she did.

[3]Of the prominent James family, Booker later served in the Chickasaw legislature. Wright, "Wapanucka Academy," 423.

In conformity with the protocol negotiated at Fort Smith, the Creeks who had taken refuge in the Choctaw and Chickasaw nations began now to bestir themselves in preparations for their return to their old homes in the Creek Nation. Preliminary thereto, however, and to pave the way for such return it was deemed best by the authorities of the Nation that a peace conference between the Southern and Northern Creeks should be held somewhere in the Creek Nation. It was arranged for such a meeting to take place at the old council ground known by the Creeks as Ue-ki-hul-we (high spring) where the National council invariably met previous to the war just closed.

Many of our people volunteered to attend this meeting, it being the first of the kind since the beginning of hostilities five years ago [before]. Sam, Dave Carr and I joined those going, and with the most of our people stopped and encamped at another good spring of water some two or more miles south of Ue-ki-hul-we. The Northern Indians failed to meet us, not a single man of them appearing for that purpose. Many of our young men bent on seeing something of our late enemy continued the journey and crossed the Arkansas below the confluence of the Verdagris river, immediately on the north banks of which were encamped the Northern Creeks among whom we numbered a few of our own relatives. Sam, Dave Carr and I were among the number who crossed the Arkansas and entered the camps of those who so lately had been our deadly enemy. We stopped at the camps of some of our relatives, these being Simpson Grayson and aunt Tility, who had shortly after the beginning of the war taken sides with the North and gone to the northern camps for protection.[4]

We remained but a day or two when we started back for Red river about one hundred and seventy miles distant. On our way back we came to the North Fork river somewhere in the near vicinity of the wagon bridge built some years since by the people of the town of Eufaula, finding it much swollen and

---

[4]The High Spring Council Ground was located in the southwest corner of present-day Muskogee County, while the reunion of Southern and Northern Creeks occurred early in Nov., 1865. David A. Carr was Grayson's brother-in-law, the husband of his sister, Adaline. See Debo, *Road to Disappearance*, 169.

entirely too deep to be forded. Our late wartime experiences had prepared us for successfully meeting such emergencies, and we at once gathered old dry cotton wood logs found on and near the banks which we lashed together with our lariats, thus improvising what served us very well as a rude form of raft, on which we securely fastened our saddles and other belongings. We then drove our horses in the raging waters, and without any mishap they swam safely across to the south bank while we were left to take our chances of following them across on the precarious craft which we had so hastily and rudely constructed. Everything being in readiness we pushed our craft out into deep water while we swam behind pushing it toward the opposite banks as best we could. The river is not wide here and we soon succeeded in landing our craft and cargo some distance below where our horses were contentedly browsing beside the banks. By hard riding we got back to our humble cabin on Red river hungry and tired out but alive.

As soon as we could, Sam and I arranged for the journey back to the old home. . . , planning for he, Pilot and I to come on first, do what we could to render our dilapidated home habitable, and repair the fences and plant a crop. We yoked up our faithful old servants, Ned and Dave, and in due time joined with Caroline and Adaline, who now were wives respectively of James Blackburn and David A. Carr. Each mustered some two or three wagons all loaded with their respective household possessions and a few negro servants and bade adieu to the Red river country. Sam and I came to our old home and of course found everything in the worst of shape; but at once addressed ourselves to the work of trying to put things to rights. Having gotten one of the houses in such condition that we could occupy it with some measure of comfort, we began to look about the farm to ascertain what was necessary there to plant and protect a corn crop. Suffice it to state here that there was much more necessary than we could possibly do.[5]

Nevertheless we went to work with a will and desperation almost, cutting poles and splitting rails all with our own

[5] The return to the Creek Nation and to the vicinity of North Fork Town probably occurred early in 1866.

hands, until in course of time we had a small farm under fence and were ready to plow. I shall not take up time or paper here in narrating the story of the terrible hardships and privations we underwent while getting our ground in readiness for seed; the difficulty of keeping ourselves in something to eat; the absence of any blacksmith's shop in the country where we could have repairs made; the nightly fear of robbers and thieves who might steal our last work horse or perhaps overpower and murder us simply for the few meagre supplies we had. All would doubtless be interesting reading but not quite to our purposes. So long had the country been abandoned that wolves had become quite numerous, as well as absolutely wild dogs that had generated from those that had been left behind by the families who had been forced to leave the country and go further South. I remember one night going out of the room I occupied on to the front porch when a wolf, which had been prowling about on the porch in quest of something to eat probably, ran away, teaching us to be on guard not only against robbers but against hungry wolves as well.

We had a family of people living a mile from us who had been on the Federal side during the war. [It] included men—two or three—who would not scruple to strangle their grandmothers for $5.00, of whom we were in constant dread. They were a gay set and drank whiskey and carried on dances there night after night where we could plainly hear their boisterous carousals. Such things never last very long, and one night when their enjoyment was at its height, the leading spirit of the festivities directed a gross insult, so we learned, against another Indian, an humble sort of a young man who had returned to the country from the south. It was too much even for one of his humility. He stepped out and was gone a few moments, when he returned with his trusty musket that had been his close companion when he had served as a Confederate soldier, and leveling it at the offender shot him dead. This case of homicide never reached any court of justice as I recall. To us this was a blessing as the place soon ceased to be the rendezvous of the people who had been assembling there to our constant perturbation.

We finally planted corn and had our affairs in fairly good shape, when it again became Sam's duty to yoke up old Dave and Ned and trek back to Red river after Mother and the rest of the children where he had left them. Sam as a young man was an excellent ox-teamster, and for that reason when there was any team-driving to be done, and our only team being oxen, it always devolved on him to do the driving. After being gone for a considerable time, he drove in one day with Mother and the children. The war was now only a grim memory and we had now at last been reunited in the old home, but with one of our number short. Our little brother, the youngest and the last of our flock, little James, had died, and had been buried near the north banks of the Red river near by my grandfather Tul-wa Tus-tun-ug-gee's grave, and was not with us.

The Creeks possessed the right of self government the same as previous to the war, and those Creeks going and sympathizing with the South, and those who went North, having now returned to the country, it became their duty unitedly to construct a government with laws for the common good of all. [This was all the more important because] the Federal government was not disposed to recognize any advantage of either party over the other, excepting the item of losses of property sustained by those who left their homes at the outbreak of hostilities and joined the fortunes of the North, which it solemnly agreed to pay.[6]

The work of reconstruction, however, proved to be a most difficult task. Those who had joined and sympathized with the North, aided by the former negro slaves of both parties who had now been declared by the Federal government to be the

[6]In Oct., 1867, at a convention which Grayson served as secretary, the united Creeks adopted a constitution and code of criminal and civil law. The constitution created a National Council composed of a House of Kings and a House of Warriors. Each town elected for four-year terms one member to the House of Kings and two members for every 200 people to the House of Warriors. It also provided for a principal chief and a second chief, both with four-year terms. The principal chief was authorized to select a private secretary, and the council was to choose a national treasurer and a national interpreter, also for four years. Grayson frequently held one of the three later posts. The nation was divided into six geographical districts with appropriate judicial and administrative officers. See Debo, *Road to Disappearance*, 180–82.

political equals of the Indians, very naturally entertained a feeling that, as they were victors in war and we coming up from the losing side, they should in the administration of government exercise superior privileges to those accorded the late adherents of the South. The intelligence and the little wealth that remained, however, was in the Southern Creeks, and this intelligence could not brook the idea of being dominated and governed by the ignorance of the northern Indians supplemented by that of their late negro slaves. The contention between the two interests was therefore at some periods so marked and bitter that the parties organized, armed and prepared for armed conflict. On one occasion the northern Creeks, some three hundred strong, marched out of the country and [took] refuge in the Comanche and Kiowa reservation, whence they were brought back by the Federal government.[7] There were occasional unavoidable hostile meetings between armed bodies of both parties, and from first to last several men were killed.

In these unfortunate disagreements between the late Northern and Southern branches of the Creeks, it is probably proper to note that the authorities of the Interior department at Washington recognized clearly that the Southern Creeks had a clear understanding of the restored relations between the Creek nation as a unit and the United States, and were endeavoring to re-establish the government on an intelligent and fair basis, and considerably in advance of the ante bellum regime. [Indeed, the Federal government] upheld the policy and contentions in the main of the Southern Creeks and the more intelligent of the Northern element who now were in sympathy with the policy advocated by Southern Creeks.

[T]his is only a hurriedly stated synopsis of the occurrence of those times, the details of which we cannot attempt to enter into for the reason that while they would doubtless be of interest to some, they would nevertheless not be strictly autobio-

[7] Grayson's reference here is to the so-called Isparhecher Rebellion, or the Green Peach War, of July, 1882. For a later reference and more detail relative to the dispute, see Chap. 10, n. 13.

Samuel Checote, principal chief of the Creeks from 1879 to 1883. *Oklahoma Historical Society.*

graphical. So what has been written is only intended to be prefatory to some things that shall hereafter be written more in line with the purposes of the work I have in hand.

Having given me extra school advantages by sending me to the Arkansas college elsewhere noted, the chiefs and headmen of the nation seemed to feel as if they had some sort of right to my services, especially as a clerk of the chiefs or the national council, and when my services were needed, exercised that right by calling and setting me to work in that capacity. Pleasant Porter and J. M. Perryman were also quite often called to act in the same work, but Porter and I were worked in this way more than anyone else.[8] At first I acted as clerk for a long time without pay, although I had the promise of pay as soon as the national affairs were so adjusted that the nation could receive the semi annual payment of the interest on its funds held in trust by the United States.

In view of prospective pay for my service and my favorable standing with the heads of our nation, my credit wherever I was known was good, and I was able soon to aid materially toward providing a livelihood for Mother and the children. I now engaged to assist Major Gray E. Scales as salesman in his business as general merchant which he conducted in a very primitive log house on the south side of the south Canadian river in the Choctaw Nation on the main traveled road to Texas. An Indian named No-co-se and family lived about one hundred yards distant while a blacksmith's shop stood near by, entitling the place according to common consent to the name.

---

[8] A brief biographical sketch of Porter is provided in n. 8, Chap. 1. Born at Choska near Muskogee in 1833, Joseph Moses Perryman attended Coweta Mission and during the Civil War served in Company A of the First Creek Regiment, C.S.A. Immediately after the war he was ordained as a Presbyterian minister, organized a Southern Presbyterian church at North Fork Town, and superintended a Presbyterian mission school (Prairie Grove, ten miles west of Eufaula) for four years after 1871. Seven years later he changed his church affiliation to that of Baptist. Perryman helped reestablish the tribal school system, served in the tribal legislature, and was elected as principal chief for a four-year term in the disputed election of 1883. Thereafter he was the president of the Creek Board of Education and superintendent of Eufaula High School. He died in Dec., 1896. See O'Beirne and O'Beirne, *Indian Territory* 1:120–21, and John Bartlett Meserve, "The Perrymans," *Chronicles of Oklahoma* 15 (June, 1937): 168–74.

of the town of Scalesville. I cannot now recall what my salary was, but I would think about $25.00 per month.[9] Along about this time the old ante bellum town of North Fork began to show symptoms of life. Ed Butler and Mr. Cox started a general merchandise business there with good prospects of success.[10] Not long subsequently Mr. G. W. Stidham and Joseph McDonald Coodey, both formerly of the old Creek Agency on the Arkansas river, erected a co-partnership establishment about fifty yards distant from Butler and Cox.[11] Not long afterward Butler sickened and died, when his widow, Mrs. Butler, engaged me to represent her interest in the store while acting in the capacity of salesmen as well. Mr. Cox also died sometime afterward, when I was engaged to serve as salesman by Mr. Stidham, who by this time had bought out Mr. Coodey's interest and was sole owner of their former co-partnership business.

While serving at Butler & Cox's and Mr. Stidham's, I met the daughter of the latter gentleman, Miss Annie Stidham, the most handsome young lady I had ever seen as I then thought, and still think. She was quiet, unobtrusive and uncomplainingly aiding her stepmother in the care of the home and her five or six children. In wealth, beauty, education and social standing, she was at that time far ahead of any Creek or other

[9] A white man married to a Choctaw woman, Gray Eagle Scales had also served as the postmaster at Tobucksy in the Choctaw Nation prior to the Civil War. He later had a successful business in Eufaula. See Grant Foreman, "Early Post Offices of Oklahoma," *Chronicles of Oklahoma* 6 (March, 1928): 5; John D. Benedict, *Muskogee and Northeastern Oklahoma* 1:493–96.

[10] A Cherokee métis but an adopted member of the Creek tribe, Edward Butler identified with the McIntosh faction and at the onset of the Civil War had recruited troops for D. N. McIntosh and Stand Watie. See "Notes and Documents," *Chronicles of Oklahoma* 44 (Aug. 1966): 322–24. "Mr. Cox" could not be identified at the time of writing.

[11] A brief account of Stidham is given in n. 5, Chap. 2. A nephew of Cherokee Chief John Ross, Joseph McDonald Coodey settled among the Creeks at North Fork Town while others in his family attained prominence among the Cherokees. Coodey's second wife was a Creek woman. After the Civil War he was a most successful businessman and was among those who helped select the townsite for present-day Eufaula in the early 1870s when the Missouri, Kansas and Texas Railroad bypassed North Fork Town. See Carolyn Thomas Foreman, "The Coody Family of Indian Territory," *Chronicles of Oklahoma* 25 (Winter, 1947): 323–41.

Georgeanna Stidham, before her marriage to G. W. Grayson, circa 1866.
Smithsonian Institution, National Anthropological Archives.

young lady within the range of my acquaintance or knowledge, and it at first impressed me that to aspire to her favor might be regarded as presumption pure and simple.[12] But looking about me I could see no one among the young men of the country, Indian or white, who for general uprightness of character had any right to claim any score of superiority over myself. Acting on this view of myself, therefore, I cultivated her acquaintance, and unlike my former experience with the Chickasaw young lady, Miss James, I formed a never-dying attachment and love for her that resulted in our marriage at her father's old cabin —they lived in a cabin then—on the 29th of July, 1869, at the west end of the lane, the marriage ceremony being performed by Rev. T. B. Ruble, a Methodist minister and former superintendent of Asbury M. L. School, when as a boy I attended school there.[13] Mrs. Mary L. Herrod, and I think Mrs. Kiziah Shaw and Mrs. Lizzie Ingram as they were then, witnessed our simple nuptials.[14]

[12]Georgeanna, or "Annie," Stidham Grayson was born Nov. 1, 1849. Her mother, G. W. Stidham's first wife, was the daughter of the noted Creek Paddy Carr. Annie died Feb. 4, 1926. See O'Beirne and O'Beirne, *Indian Territory* 1:134.

[13]See Chap 2, n. 8.

[14]Mary Lewis Herrod was educated at Tullahassee Mission and became the first woman to teach in Creek national schools. Her husband, Goliah Herrod, was a full-blood Creek, an active Baptist layman, and at one time superintendent of Creek public schools. After her husband's death Mary Herrod operated a hotel in Eufaula. Her sister, Kiziah Shaw, was also a teacher in the Creek public schools at North Fork Town. She later married Moty Tiger, a chief of the Creeks early in the twentieth century. Lizzie Ingram was Elizabeth Stidham Ingram, the sister of G. W. Stidham and the aunt of Annie. Lizzie had attended Coweta and Tullahassee missions and was herself a teacher in the Creek schools. See Carolyn Thomas Foreman, "Two Notable Women of the Creek Nation," *Chronicles of Oklahoma* 35 (Autumn, 1957): 315–28, and Lanford, "North Fork to Eufaula, 1836–1907," p. 81.

CHAPTER NINE

National Treasurer

THE FOLLOWING WINTER, Judge Stidham as he had often done before, went to Washington, D.C. in the capacity of a representative of the nation before the departments of the government, being elected thereto by the Creek council, leaving me and one Tip Hume, a relative of his wife, in charge of his business. On his return after completing his mission and the business was turned over to him, we removed away from North Fork to Mother's, some three or more miles to the old home where I was reared, and where we lived perhaps a year.[1]

While we were living here I was planning for a home of our own. Finding that D. B. Whitlow wanted to sell his old country home and farm of some 15 or 20 acres together with a few hogs and cattle at what seemed to me to be a very reasonable valuation, I determined to buy the property if I could. I went to my uncle Watt Grayson and borrowed the money, $500.00, and paid for the place, and as soon as possible prepared for house keeping and removed to our new home. The home was only new in the sense of being different from and not the same place we had lived at previously, and in a new neighborhood.[2]

[1] Grayson and his bride must have lived at his mother's place, situated south of present-day Eufaula, during the period from 1870 to 1871. See Chap. 2 above.

[2] An intermarried white man, David B. Whitlow was a most successful merchant in North Fork Town and later in Eufaula. Grayson's move to the Whitlow place probably occurred in 1871. Watt Grayson's affluence was relatively well known. In Nov., 1873, he was robbed of $30,000 in gold and $2,000 in U.S. currency by James H. Reed, W. D. Wilder, and Marion Dickens, telling of the

This home consisted of a double log cabin, the logs of which they were constructed being mostly of the black jack timber. The openings between the logs were chinked and daubed with exceedingly red clay. These two rooms were each probably 14 feet by 15, with large fire places, the chimneys being constructed of timbers re-enforced with stone and clay to prevent them from burning when fires were kindled in them. This was certainly a most humble home, but did not impress us as being strikingly so, for we had not so long since lived in just such structures as well as seen others live in what were called dug-outs, when refugeeing in the Choctaw and Chickasaw nations. We even had no yard fence, and any stock that might be roaming about the neighborhood, cattle, ponies or hogs came right up to our doors if they so chose.

Sometime previous to this, after using me in a somewhat lengthy apprenticeship in the affairs of our nation, as Clerk for the chiefs, council and convention, I was by the national council elected treasurer of the Nation.[3] [I] was occupying this responsible position when I was living in my little double log cabin on the farm. My recollection of this service is that I occupied the office two successive terms of four years. As has been stated, the Creeks who had espoused the cause of the Confederacy and those who joined with the North were in a continual turmoil. It came about that some of those of the southern people who were not altogether satisfied with the policy and methods of their own party affected to sympathize with the northern party, while some others who did not endorse the contentions of the northern party, nevertheless for ulterior reasons, ranged themselves with them. These endeav-

money's location only after he had been dangled from a hangman's rope six times. See Foreman, "North Fork Town," 91 and 107n, and Contract between Wm. H. Anderson and Paine-Grafton, Washington, D.C., Oct. 17, 1877, Misc. Section X, Creek Nation Papers, Manuscript Division, Oklahoma State Historical Society.

[3] Grayson was elected national treasurer in Oct., 1869, to complete the unexpired term of his predecessor and then served two more four-year terms until Oct., 1879. For his services he received $300 per year. G. W. Grayson bond, Nov., 1869, #39314, and Samuel C. Checote, Okmulgee, to J. Q. Tufts, Dec. 18, 1879, #39334, Treasurer Records, Creek Nation Papers, Manuscript Division, Oklahoma Historical Society.

The Grayson children and Georgeanna, circa 1884. Left to right: Orleana, Washington, Eloise, Walter, Tsianina, and Mrs. G. W. Grayson. *Courtesy of David Hansard.*

ored to bring about a condition of affairs which if it did not give control of the moneys of the Creek treasury to the northern party, would at least turn over the control and disbursement of a large portion of it to them.[4]

This was being successfully resisted by the southern party when the U.S. Indian Agent received two large consignments of money from Washington for disbursement to the Creeks. One amount was one hundred thousand dollars, which amount he was instructed by the Washington government to pay out to individual Creek citizens who in the late war had been loyal to the Federal government, to reimburse them for losses of property sustained during the war by reason of their loyalty to said Federal government. In this the southern party had no interest, as they had opposed that government, and at that time laid no claims to any. The other installment of money brought by the

---

[4]For a full discussion of the political problems besetting the Creeks in the post–Civil War era, see Debo, *Road to Disappearance,* chaps. 6 and 7.

Indian Agent was the annual interest on the National funds of the nation, and was used in defraying the expenses of the Creek government and schools. It was usually paid to the Creek treasurer, who disbursed it in accordance with the will of the national council. I have forgotten the amount of this, but it was as I believe between seventy and ninety thousand dollars.[5]

As treasurer I went on horseback to the Agency to receive and convey this fund to Okmulkee where our national council was in session, there to be disbursed or held as it might direct. Arriving at the Agency, I found the little town alive with the Indians and negroes of the northern party who had gathered there in large numbers to participate in the disbursement by the Indian Agent of the one hundred thousand dollars on their claims for losses sustained by reason of the late war. Among the assemblage was Col. Timothy Barnett who in the latter part of the late war was my regimental colonel, but who now was acting with the northern Indians, our late enemy. His wife, Mary Benson, was my relative as has elsewhere been explained, and during the war we served in the same regiment and were the best of friends. But since he elected to cast his political lot with those who had been our enemy and were now in active opposition to us, I could not help entertaining a feeling of unfriendliness and never sought his company.[6]

People who saw me among the throng at the agency knew well that I must be there for the purpose of receiving the national funds. I said nothing about my business, however, but was planning how to receive and get away with so much

[5]The payment to which Grayson here refers apparently occurred in 1870. Capt. F. A. Field was the U.S. agent, his offices being northwest of present-day Muskogee in the midst of a community of Creek freedmen. Debo, *Road to Disappearance*, 189.

[6]Grandson of Timpoochee Barnard, an ally of William McIntosh, Col. Timothy Barnett had commanded Grayson's regiment in the second battle of Cabin Creek. He had also been selected as the first treasurer of the tribe under the constitution of 1867. A resident of Wewoka District, where he lived with Mary Benson, Barnett had a second wife in the Greenleaf settlements. After killing a suitor of the second woman, he himself was killed in 1873 by lighthorsemen who were members of an opposing political faction. Debo, *Road to Disappearance*, 202–203. See also Chap. 1, n. 12.

money unobserved by persons in this vast crowd who might gladly follow and kill me on the road and carry it away. While I was mingling with the people, a great many of whom were old acquaintances, I was approached by this same Timothy Barnett. Beckoning me to one side, [he] said in confidence,

Captain you and I have served together in war and elsewhere for a long time, and between us personally there exists no enmity although we are somewhat estranged in our present political affiliations. I approach you now as I feel that I ought to, to say to you some things which may serve as a warning and possibly be of benefit to you. I am in the confidence of these northern Indians who have assembled here in such large numbers, and they, as well as others who know of the office you occupy, know that you have come to carry away the national funds to Okmulkee, and are free in declaring that you shall never reach there with them. Nothing is said as to how you will be prevented from safely reaching the council with the money, and I only tell you this so that you may be on your guard and devise such ways and means for the safety of yourself and the funds in your charge as you shall deem best. You, of course, might secure for your protection on the way a strong guard of men; or you might quietly effect your departure with the funds at some least expected hour of the night; or take some little known by-path to Okmulkee, but I shall not advise you to pursue any particular course; I simply am doing what I conceive to be my duty to you.

I thanked Colonel Barnett for his friendly act in this instance, and assured him that I should try to profit by it.

My plans for getting away from this place and arriving safely in Okmulkee with the funds were already shaped in my own mind, and I doubt that the suggestions of the colonel made an iota of difference in them. As I had intended doing, I quietly inquired if there were any of the Lighthorsemen of the Creek government on the ground whom I might impress into service as guide over an unusual route to Okmulkee.[7] I was

[7] "Lighthorsemen" were law enforcement officers appointed by the chiefs, with a tradition that dated back to the 1790s and Alexander McGillivray's "constables" and Benjamin Hawkins's specially appointed warriors. See Carolyn

referred to Johnson Kennard, a man whose integrity and cool courage in time of danger was often a subject of remark. Although not acquainted with him, I hunted him up and found him to be a man of medium build and height with a good face, about 45 years of age, but had the appearance of having a mixture of negro blood in his veins. He conversed altogether in Indian. I informed him of the object I had in approaching him, and asked if he knew of any by-path that is [was?] not now being traveled much by the public, which we could travel and reach Okmulkee safely with the big wad of money that I would have turned over to me [that] night. He said yes, that it was an easy matter, if we were not picked up on our way, to travel a trail or path that went out of the town through the hills and the prairies directly to the Ue-ki-hul-we.[8] Once here it was no trick at all to continue on safely to Okmulkee.

"Very well then," said I, " . . . you await me here until I go with my saddle bags and receive the money and return, when we will immediately leave with you as pilot. I shall depend upon you." It was some little time after dark when we were talking, and I went away and after quite a considerable time consumed in counting the money, I returned and found Kennard at his post. Without a word I put my saddle pockets across my saddle and mounted my faithful animal, [and] when Kennard in a low voice asked "Are you ready?" I answered "Yes I'm ready; lead the way." We rode along picking our way through the many people passing to and fro in a rather unconcerned manner until we got out of the town, when we urged our animals along at a much faster gait, but preserving a si-

---

Thomas Foreman, "The Light-Horsemen of Indian Territory," *Chronicles of Oklahoma* 34 (Spring, 1956): 32–43.

[8] Ue-ki-hul-we hill is the location of the High Spring Council Ground situated in the southeastern corner of present-day Okmulgee County. Rather than strike a course due west toward the settlement at Okmulgee, as would a modern driver, Grayson and Kennard went south and west out of Muskogee. In 1879 a traveler over a similar trail reported that the prairie was covered with grass "as high as the horses' backs, brown, untouched, waving and dimpling in the wind." Stems from a bundle of wild grasses taken from this same area in 1880 measured from seven to nine feet high. See Debo, *Road to Disappearance*, 260–61.

lence as between ourselves lest our talk drown out the noise of approaching pursuers and put us in their power.

In this quiet, noiseless way we continued our course in single file until we had reached and traveled far enough into the prairie to be able to discern even in the dark any object the size of a man or horse for a considerable distance away. We [then] slackened our gait and congratulated ourselves on our signal success in getting out of town without pursuit. We continued our course through what seemed a trackless prairie and until we could not muster further subjects of conversation and the desire for sleep began to assert its claims. We combatted this for a time, but nature in me finally called an armistice, and seeing a lone elm tree a considerable distance to the east of our trail I called to Kennard that we turn out to that tree and lie down by it and sleep until day light. This we did, I placing my saddle bags with the money in them at the root of the tree which I used for a pillow, and sleeping the sleep of the just and secure, while Kennard slept only a few steps away.

The situation was unique indeed. Here was the treasurer of the Creek nation with between seventy and ninety thousand dollars in his custody asleep in a vast prairie with a solitary companion whom he never had personally known until the last four or five hours. Kennard could have turned on me during the night and with a club or my own pistol despatched me on the spot, and taken the money and at his own leisure get out of the country. Such fears had no place in my thoughts, however, and indeed there was still much of that old fashioned honesty and high respect for personal honor in those days that fully justified me in doing then with an ordinary unchristian Indian officer that which I would not now do with the ordinary christian sunday school superintendent of the white race. Times and people certainly have changed.

Morning dawned and found us with our horses alive, refreshed and ready for the road, with all of our money intact. Saddling up we continued our course and climbing the Ue-ki-hul-we hill we rode up to the home of an old Creek Indian lady who had lived there even long previous to the war, well known to many by the name of aunt Hannah, where we called for

Eloise Grayson Smock, Grayson's daughter, circa 1895. *Courtesy of David Hansard.*

breakfast. She declared she had nothing that was fit for us to eat and could not accommodate us. Kennard, however, explained our own unfortunate circumstances and willingness to accept thankfully just anything that she would prepare [and] insisted that she give us something for breakfast. She said then that if we could eat such as she had, we were welcome to it. So saying, she placed upon the table a dish of the dark leaves of cabbages which seemed to have been chopped up quite fine and stewed down until completely cooked and which she had already prepared. This with a teacup of water completed that which for me was by far the most meagre and scanty breakfast . . . that I have ever partaken of in all my life. The cabbages, however, had been seasoned with exactly the proper quantity of salt, and was quite to my taste; and adhering to the peculiar style of cooking, it could not have been better prepared. Anyway, we know [knew?] that the good old lady did the best she could for us, and my recollection is that I settled for both of our breakfasts, when continuing our journey without any further apprehensions of trouble, we arrived at the capital—Okmulkee—at about high noon, where the chief Checote and others congratulated me on my safe arrival with the Creek funds.[9]

This was one incident of my official life as the treasurer during the time I lived on my farm in the little double log cabin where we were in constant dread of attack from robbers who might, without much trouble, have attacked me at any time and gotten away with such amount of the public funds as happened to be on hand at the time. Then there was the other danger of being attacked and probably killed for money that I did not have. The robbers might be very ignorant men and, only knowing that the treasurer was the officer who is supposed always to have large amounts of money at his home, might come and kill or greatly abuse me at any time even when there was not a dollar in my custody, as was most generally the case. This constantly present danger was trying on one's nerve, but of this latter I was yet well supplied and kept up a bold front and a close watch for possible trouble.

[But] on one night . . . my equanimity was considerably jarred; in fact jarred as I never had it exercised before. At this time I happened to have in the house several thousand dollars of the public moneys and was somewhat apprehensive of possible attack. We had had a snow storm and the ground was covered with some four or five inches of snow. It was night, and the log fire I had built in the great chimney fireplace had burnt down and gave out a very faint light. [S]ometime in the night about ten or eleven o'clock perhaps, we were awakened

[9] Born in 1819 and removed to Indian Territory in 1829, Samuel Checote was a full blood associated with the Lower Towns and the McIntosh faction. He was an early convert to Methodism and once fled the Creek Nation to escape religious persecution. During the Civil War, Checote rose to the rank of colonel while serving with the First Regiment of Creek Mounted Volunteers, C.S.A. He was elected first chief of the Creeks under the new constitution of 1867 and served two terms, or until 1875. He served another four-year term between 1879 and 1883. He died the year after he left office. Although Checote lived on the Deep Fork in the western portion of present-day Okmulgee County, the town of Checotah was named for him. See John Bartlett Meserve, "Chief Samuel Checote, with Sketches of Chiefs Locher Harjo and Ward Coachman," *Chronicles of Oklahoma* 16 (Dec., 1938): 402–403, 407–408.

by the noise made by animals trampling on the yielding snow and which seemed to be coming from several directions toward our house. I did not like this at all.

At once [I] got out of bed and covered up the fire with ashes so that it gave out no light by which anyone on the outside could see me or my movements. The snow had become encrusted on the surface but not sufficiently so to uphold the weight of a horse, and what we heard were [was] evidently the walking of horses which broke through the crusted snow, and causing the noise made by one animal [to] sound, especially to an excited imagination, like that made by several. These sounds were coming too from all directions toward our house. We now were in our own minds fully satisfied that the attack we had so long feared . . . was tonight to become a reality. I hurriedly slipped on some of my clothing, got my pistol— almost everybody kept one in those days—and instructing Mrs. Grayson to remain quietly in bed, posted myself to one side of the door intending in breathless expectation to shoot the first person who should break the door down and attempt to enter the cabin. There being no fence to prevent them, the intruders came up to within two or three feet of the walls of our cabin, occasioning no noise save that made by tramping on and breaking through the crusted snow. So near me on the outside stood some of them that I imagined I could hear their breathing while they stood very quietly for a moment, which seemed hours to me. I know of no time in life when I was so greatly alarmed and so I desperately determined to make it a costly victory for the intruders if they should win in the fight which I expected would be on within the next minute. With the partial light afforded by the whiteness of the snow without, which would enable me to discern forms and movements, and the complete darkness within shielding me from view, I had some advantage over the attacking party. I intended making full use of it.

Just then when breathless excitement was at its highest tension, we plainly heard the noise when made on the outside by a cow licking the clay with which the walls of our cabin were snugly daubed, as has already been elsewhere stated. These innocent beasts belonging to myself and others in the neighborhood had often gathered near the house and tonight it seemed good to them while out for a nocturnal prowl to call and see what was doing at the Grayson manse. The hour being a particularly quiet one, [they] came up nearer than it had been their wont, and thus for a few minutes that seemed many hours occasioned untold agony to us.

As a matter of course it was never my intention to remain in the log cabins that we occupied, and my efforts tho slow were continuously being exerted in the interest of better structure for a home. Pine lumber for building purposes was too costly, so I conceived the idea of building another and better log house some ten rods away northwest in an elevated grove of tall trees where everything would be entirely new and built as nearly as I wanted it, as my limited means would permit. For this purpose, I with my own hands and hired help chopped and felled trees in the neighboring woods and hauled them to a little saw mill that Col. D. N. McIntosh had established on the banks of the North Fork river where Walter Grayson's little daughter Nonie's allotment and farm now is.[10] [There] they were sawed on two opposite sides as I directed, thus forming material of which, if properly constructed, log houses with smooth walls could be built.

Of this material Billy and Dave Ingram built for me a double house with a porch extending the entire length of the east side of the structure.[11] Some eight or ten feet from the house on the west we had our kitchen, and our old fashioned dug and walled well was sunk some fifteen or twenty feet to the south. The rooms were ceiled inside with pine lumber, canvassed and papered, while the interstices of the walls on the outside were pointed with lime mortar, and one room the south, provided

[10]Grayson here refers to an 80-acre allotment of his granddaughter, Lenore, located in the southeast quarter of Sec. 16, T 10 N, R 16 E, on the south bank of the North Fork River some three miles west and four miles north of Eufaula, at present inundated by the lake. See Chap. 7, n. 1, and the Creek Allotment Rolls, Records of the Dawes Commission, Manuscript Division, Oklahoma Historical Society.

[11]The Ingrams were probably the cousins or uncles of Grayson's wife. See Chap. 8, n. 14.

with a chimney made of squared stones. Thus after a long wait, much of the waiting being consequent on the slow motions of the builders, I had succeeded in providing my family with what was by far the best and most sightly home of any in the country for many miles around.

While I had thus gotten myself in very good shape, having now a good home, a good office, several cattle and hogs, my brother Sam induced me to aid him as salesman in the general merchandise store of Major G. E. Scales at Eufaula, where I worked for a time coming home on Saturday evening of each week.[12] I had at this time three children, Lena, Mabel and Annette.[13] Mother who was living at the old home near Eufaula came often to spend a few days with us, and was a great favorite with our children. On one such occasion she came on one of her visits to us and finding that her aunt Leah, colonel Chilly McIntosh's wife, living in the near neighborhood was quite ill, went to assist in nursing her, where she remained until her death. Returning to our home quite exhausted by the anxiety and care she had experienced in attending the sick, she too became ill of a like ailment as that which caused the death of her aunt. Our youngest child, Annette, also became ill, and before many days died. Then in only a very few days thereafter Mother also died. These were dark days for us.

Brother and I finally, with uncle Watt Grayson's aid, bought out the old proprietor Scales, who was quite an old man and hardly fit to meet the demands of active business. With this change in my relations . . . [and] being now joint proprietor with Sam and Edmond Grayson of the mercantile business now running under the firm name of Grayson Bros., it seemed necessary that I should move my family and effects to town where I could be constantly with the business.

Consequently I was planning how I might best make the removal from my farm to town and in fact had started to build a

[12]See Chap. 8, n. 9.
[13]Grayson's first child, Lena—actually Orlena—was born Aug. 4, 1870. She married W. H. Sanger, had a home in Eufaula, but died June 28, 1892. Mabel was born Jan. 16, 1872; she died Oct. 26, 1888. Annette was born Dec. 28, 1874. See Grayson family scrapbook in the possession of David Hansard, Dover, Tennessee.

Wash Grayson, son of G. W. Grayson and chief of the Creeks, in about 1917. *Courtesy of David Hansard.*

home when one night a serious misfortune overtook me which
had the effect of hastening my movements. Mrs. Grayson
had been confined and delivered of a boy baby (now Walter
Clarence) and was yet in bed not expecting to leave it for a
week or more longer, when during the early part of the night
and when I and the two little girls, Lena and Mabel, were
asleep, fire broke out in the north room which was unoccupied
and forced us all out into a slow drizzling rain.[14] The baby was
but eight days old but Mrs. Grayson was forced to leave her
bed and go out into the rain while I was exerting every effort
to save such of our household effects as I could handle, from
the destroying flames. At the old cabins we lately lived in
[there] lived a negro renter and family, Willis Rose by name,
who was working our farm, who hearing our cries of distress
came to our aid and succeeded in saving a portion of our supply of bacon that we had in the burning smoke house. Thus
the home we had waited for so long and worked and saved and
denied ourselves so patiently in order to realize, went up and
disappeared in smoke inside of a few hours and we were
houseless.

We repaired to the old cabins, our former home where our
negro renters were living, and remained overnight. On the following morning I borrowed a pair of shoes many numbers too
large for me from Willis and putting them on rode to town to
arrange for the care of my family. Securing the necessary
conveyance, we hauled ourselves and the few effects saved
from the fire out to the old home of my early youth, which
since Mother's death was being occupied by Pilot, my brother
younger than Sam. Sometime in about June of that year our
house in town having been completed, we moved into it and
have lived here owning no other home ever since.[15]

---

[14] Since Walter Clarence Grayson was born on March 8, 1876, the fire must
have been on March 16, 1876.

[15] The move occurred in June, 1876. The town, of course, was Eufaula. Encouraged by a $1,000 subsidy raised by G. W. and Sam Grayson, G. W. Stidham,
G. E. Scales, D. B. Whitlow, and Joseph Coodey, the Missouri, Kansas and
Texas Railroad had chosen the site of the community for one of its stations and
had completed construction of tracts to it by March, 1872. Eufaula became a
major trading center thereafter, quickly eclipsing and soon replacing North Fork

Being still national treasurer, I conducted that business in the office of our firm here, with none of the fears that had me so constantly in dread when I lived on the farm. The national council besides had purchased a little old-fashioned iron safe of Sanford Perryman, which as compared with the elaborate modern burglar-proof time-lock affairs we see now in most business offices was not much safer than an ordinary kitchen safe.[16] In this I kept the national moneys when there were any to be kept, along with documents pertaining to the business of the treasurer's office. On a certain night when I had no suspicions whatever of anything like robbery, the store was broken into and this safe robbed of something over twelve hundred dollars. The national council was either in session at the time or soon thereafter, as I distinctly recall that I rendered an official report of the misfortune in a short time after the occurrence to that body, which promptly passed a resolution holding me responsible for the loss. This I resisted, holding that the money had been taken from the particular receptacle furnished me by the nation, which was presumed by all to be proof against just such robbery as had occurred; that I had placed the money in this safe, keeping it in as safe a building as I had; that no one ever contemplated that I should stand guard over the national safe night and day; that what had occurred came not because of any negligence whatever, on my part, and therefore I refused to make the loss good.[17]

Town. The principal commercial and residential sections of the old town lay east of the tracks and the present new town. See Benedict, *Muskogee and Northeastern Oklahoma* 1:495–96; Lanford, "North Fork To Eufaula, 1836–1907," p. 79.

[16] Born at Sodom in 1834, Sanford Perryman attended Coweta and Tullahassee mission schools and was a proficient interpreter and translator of the Creek language. He supported the South early during the Civil War, but changed his allegiance in 1862 to the Union. Perryman represented Loyalist Creeks in the negotiations following the war, helped to write the constitution of 1867, superintended Tullahassee, was a member of the House of Warriors, and served his people as delegate to Washington on several occasions. He died in 1876. Meserve, "The Perrymans," 174.

[17] Grayson reported on Aug. 8, 1877, that the safe was robbed of $1,276.75 "sometime ago" and that he had learned that one Robert Sewell had been seen with a sum of money filling the description of that which had been taken. See G. W. Grayson, Eufaula, to Ward Coachman, Aug. 8, 1877, #39329, and

Some years afterward Albert P. McKellop had the national council to pass an act authorizing him to institute suit in the Supreme Court of the Creek nation against all persons who were in arrears with the nation with a fee for himself I think of 25% of all amounts recovered. Now there were many persons so in arrears who had no valid reasons for failing to settle; some who had collected large moneys for the account of the nation but failed to turn them in or render any report of them whatever; others who had forfeited their bonds to the nation, against whom, as it seems to me, he would have no trouble in obtaining a verdict, yet he passed all these and singled me out and instituted proceedings in the Supreme court against me. My contention was sustained by that body.[18]

McKellop seemed thereupon to regard himself as down and out, as he never took up any other case, and there was never more heard of the proposed prosecutions. Some of the other persons whom he could have arraigned for settlement with the nation were, as I understood, particular friends of his. I have though it might be possible that he intended to reap good fees out of the cases against me and a few others to whom he sustained no special relations of friendship or political sympathy, and compromise with those friends to whom he felt himself under obligations on such easy terms as would not seriously affect them. Be that as it may, it is true that no further suits under the law were ever instituted by Mr. McKellop. It seemed much as if the act he had passed was conceived specifically for

Grayson, Eufaula, to Coachman, March 20, 1878, #39330, Treasurer Records, Creek Nation Papers, Manuscript Division, Oklahoma Historical Society.

[18] Albert Pike McKellop, whose grandmother was a Perryman, was a resident of Muskogee, secretary of the Muskogee Fair Association, and active in tribal politics. He served as attorney general of the Creeks, and in 1893 compiled a comprehensive law code for the tribe. The following year he and Grayson represented the Creeks on a mission to Washington. In 1900 he helped negotiate the Creek Allotment Agreement.

The act authorizing election of an attorney, in this case McKellop, to institute suit was passed on Nov. 3, 1893. The case involving Grayson apparently came before the Creek Supreme Court in June, 1894. See O'Beirne and O'Beirne, *Indian Territory* 1:231–32; Debo, *Road to Disappearance*, 260, 313, 348; and *Acts and Resolutions of the National Council of the Muskogee Nation of 1893 and 1899, inclusive*, 11–12.

the purpose of injuring me, and when it failed to do that, he had no further use for it. After my last term of office as treasurer, I never aspired to the position any more but was elected by the Coweta town one of its members to the House of Warriors of the National council, where I served for some three or more terms of four years each.[19]

[19] See Chap. 8, n. 6. That the traditional town and matrilineal social structure of the Creeks remained viable after the Civil War is suggested by Grayson's election. Although he was a physical resident of Eufaula, he represented in the national council the Coweta town that was situated some 65 miles north and west of his own home. According to Creek tribal records, Grayson's service in the House of Warriors encompassed at least the years 1883 to 1891; he was also elected as an additional member of the House of Warriors from Coweta Town in September, 1897. A contemporary secondary source reported that in 1892 he was "recently reelected" to the House for a term that extended until 1895. Grayson was also an unsuccessful candidate for second chief of the Creeks in 1899. See election returns from Coweta, Sept. 3, 1883, #29394, and election returns for Sept. 5, 1899, #29646, Election Records; Certificate of election signed by Coweta Micco, Dec. 3, 1887, #32942, and Certificate of election, Sept. 2, 1897, #33455, National Council Records, Creek Nation Papers, Manuscript Division, Oklahoma Historical Society; and O'Beirne and O'Beirne, *Indian Territory* 1:134.

CHAPTER TEN

The Passing of a Nation

DURING THESE YEARS I often rendered service as representative of the Creek nation in international Indian councils and conventions. For some three or four years I served as Clerk of the Indian International council provided for in the treaties of 1866, under appointment of C. Delano who at that time was Secretary of the Interior of the United States.[1] These councils met each year at Okmulkee, where there was need of much interpreting of remarks of the representatives of various tribes,

[1] Known as the Okmulgee Council because of its place of meeting, the Indian International Council held its first meeting in 1870. It was attended by representatives of the Five Tribes, the Osages, and some of the smaller tribes of Indian Territory. A constitution was written that provided for a governor, a general assembly composed of a senate and house of representatives, and a court system. The Creeks and the Choctaws, as well as some of the smaller tribes, ratified the document, but other Indian groups refused, fearing that the Okmulgee constitution might result in a formal territorial government and ultimately the loss of their land. Although the federal government suspended appropriations to pay its expenses in 1874, the council continued to meet on a regular basis through the 1880s, but primarily with Five Tribes representation. Grayson apparently served as secretary between 1870 and 1875. Columbus Delano, a native of Ohio, a Republican, and a two-term member of the U.S. House of Representatives from that state, was secretary of the interior from 1870 to 1875. See Allen G. Applen, "An Attempted Indian State Government: The Okmulgee Constitution in Indian Territory, 1870–1876," *Kansas Quarterly* 3 (Fall, 1971): 89–99; *Biographical Directory of the American Congress, 1774–1961*, 796; "Journal of the Adjourned Session of First General Council of the Indian Territory," *Chronicles of Oklahoma* 3 (April, 1925): 33–44; and Muriel H. Wright, "A Report to the General Council at Okmulgee in 1873," *Chronicles of Oklahoma* 34 (Spring, 1956): 8–16.

Delegates to the International Council assembled at the Creek Capital Building in Okmulgee, 1878. Thirty-four tribes were represented. Grayson served as secretary of the council. *Oklahoma Historical Society.*

the remarks of one speaker having some times to be interpreted to four or five different tribes by as many different interpreters, which rendered the transaction of business very tedious. I invariably interpreted for the Creek representation rendering the English into Creek, and sometime the Creek into English. My complexion and person having so much the appearance of the white man that I could speak the Indian as I did appeared decidedly striking to the wild Indians who attended these councils. The fact that I was Indian and spoke the language and was also secretary of this great Indian body appointed by the Secretary of the Interior at Washington, impressed the simple representatives of some of those tribes with the belief that I must be a person of very considerable importance and fully entitled to their confidence. Whenever I met any of them either in Washington or elsewhere as I often did years afterwards, they would in perfect confidence state to me their business and ask my advice.

On one occasion a very old man, member of the Kickapoo tribe, whom I did not know personally, rode horseback all the way from his reservation nearly a hundred miles distant to my home in Eufaula to consult me as I supposed in relation to his tribal affairs. He was alone and carried an official envelope addressed to me, but the little that I found written by somebody within gave me no clue to the poor old fellow's wants, while his dense ignorance of the English and mine of Kickapoo prevented the shedding of any light on the object of his visit, and he was forced to return without accomplishing anything.[2]

On another occasion the Wichitaws [Wichitas] who had for quite a good while also been very friendly with me, wrote for me to visit the tribe, it being located on the north side of Washitaw [Washita] river from the town of Anadarko, on a small ever running stream named Sugar Creek. The tribe desired to lease their reservation to me for pasturing cattle, a business much in vogue at that time. I went to see what could be done, not expecting to engage in pasturing cattle but hoping to assist these old friends of mine in negotiating with cattlemen of Texas who would treat them fairly. Many men had tried to contract with them for pasture privileges on their reservation, but they were afraid to attempt a deal with white men and hence refused to contract with anyone.[3]

[2] Assigned to the tribe in 1874, the Kickapoo reservation was just west of the Sac and Fox domain, was bordered on the north by the Deep Fork River and on the south by the North Canadian, and was just east of the so-called Unassigned Lands. The 100,000-acre reserve was situated in present-day southern Lincoln and northern Pottawatomie counties. See A. M. Gibson, *The Kickapoos: Lords of the Middle Border*, 257.

[3] The 743,000-acre Wichita and Caddo reservation, assigned to the tribes in 1872, extended north of the Washita River to the South Canadian and west from the Chickasaw domain to that of the Cheyenne and Arapaho. It encompassed the northern two-thirds of present Caddo and parts of Grady, Canadian, and Blaine counties. See Muriel H. Wright, *A Guide to the Indian Tribes of Oklahoma*, 260.

Ranching in western Oklahoma had its genesis in the cattle drives out of Texas, which in the 1870s sent some 3,000,000 head to markets in Kansas. To enhance profits by being closer to the railheads, cattlemen as individuals and as groups during the next decade leased rangeland from the different tribes of western Indian Territory. On the Comanche and Kiowa reservation leasing began as early as 1881. In 1882 the Cheyennes and Arapahos leased their 3,000,000 acres as pasture for 200,000 head of cattle for $60,000 per annum. The following year the Cherokees leased their 6,500,000-acre Outlet for $100,000 per year as range

On my invitation Joseph M. Perryman accompanied me on this venture, and when we reached the town of Anadarko, we deemed that courtesy and respect for the office of U.S. Indian Agent required, as we were expecting to do business with the Indians of the agency, that we visit and pay our respects to that official and apprise him of the fact that we were going to meet and confer with the wards of his agency. We met the Indian Agent and he said we were welcome to visit the Indians and confer with them as much as we liked. He asked if our business with them had any relation to their lands. When we told him it did, he remarked that others had tried to effect deals with those Indians involving their lands and had invariably failed, and we were welcome to effect any land deals with them that we could. He did not know that any of us had been sent for by the Indians and that we were well known to them, as we kept this to ourselves.[4]

We went to the Indians' encampment, where, when our arrival was heralded throughout the camp, we were received with genuine aboriginal hospitality. In a day or two the Indians through their council appointed certain of their number to negotiate with us and we soon signed a lease contract with them for pasture privileges on hundreds of thousands of acres of the Wichitaw reservation, and returned. When afterwards the U.S. Indian Agent found what had been done, he was said to have been quite angry at the Indians for what they had done, and declared that had he known of our object in meeting the Indians he would have had us arrested and put off of the reservation.[5]

---

for 300,000 cattle. A. M. Gibson, *Oklahoma: A History of Five Centuries,* 2d. ed., 169–70.

[4]For Joseph M. Perryman, see Chap. 8, n. 8. The Wichita and Caddo tribes had been placed under the jurisdiction of the Comanche and Kiowa agency in 1878, and the combined administrative headquarters was located in Anadarko. If the analysis below is correct (n. 5), the agent mentioned by Grayson was W. D. Meyers. See William T. Hagan, *United States–Comanche Relations: The Reservation Years,* 140, 169.

[5]Grayson's and Perryman's lease with the Wichitas was apparently negotiated in the spring of 1889. Indian Territory newspapers reported a rumor that Grayson and Perryman had secured a power of attorney from the Wichitas to sell their lands, a rumor that prompted the Bureau of Indian Affairs in Washington to

On another occasion ex-governor and ex-congressman Throckmorton of Texas, a most estimable gentleman as all who knew him will gladly testify, was making an effort to obtain the attorneyship of the Caddo tribe to prosecute certain claims against the government at Washington for them, and had either written or visited them for the purpose of effecting a contract to do that work. Just what occurred in the conference the ex-governor had with them I do not know, but suspect that they postponed action with the promise of making some investigations and answering him later on the subject. I remember receiving a letter from the chief of the Caddos wherein he stated that a white man from Texas claiming to be acquainted with me, named either "Frogmountain or Jackmarten," just which he did not know, who desired the contract for the attorneyship for the Caddo tribe, and before closing with him he wanted to know of me if the man in question was one to be depended on or not. I returned the highest testimonial in governor Throckmorton's favor, as I was well satisfied that the Indians could not get in safer hands. What was done I have never heard, while the governor has long since been dead.[6]

While acting for my own nation as delegate in the city of Washington, I have been time and again written by chief Moses Keokuk of the Sac and Foxes, another blanket tribe, to include his tribe in any measure or movement that I was trying to effect with the government for the protection of the interests of my own people. I only introduce the facts as proofs of the statement previously made, that through my secretaryship of the Indian International council at Okmulkee, I came to be

inquire into the matter. A copy of the criticized power of attorney has not been found, but it probably was the lease agreement to which Grayson here refers. See *Muskogee Phoenix,* July 25, 1889, 4; *Indian Arrow,* July 25, 1889, 2; Acting Commissioner Belt, Washington, to W. D. Meyers, Aug. 30, 1889, Foreign Relation Records, Kiowa Papers, Manuscript Division, Oklahoma Historical Society.

[6]Once residents of northeastern Texas, the Caddos shared a reservation with Wichitas. A resident of McKinney, Texas, James W. Throckmorton was governor of the state in 1866 and 1867 and from 1875 to 1879, and between 1883 and 1887 he was a member of the U.S. House of Representatives from Texas. Past members of congress frequently sought to represent the claims of Indian tribes upon the United States before various agencies of the government. *Biographical Directory of the American Congresses, 1774–1961,* 1713–14.

regarded by the wild or blanket Indians as a friend and person of more than ordinary importance.[7]

During the years these International councils were being held in Okmulkee, all manner of efforts were made by people of the surrounding states—Kansas in particular—to bring influences to bear on the authorities at Washington to cause the government to violate its treaties with the Creeks and the other sister tribes and open up the Oklahoma country to white settlement. The Indians opposed this and insisted that it remain for future settlement thereon of other Indians as had been expressly stipulated in solemn treaties. In order if possible to force the government to open the country to white settlement against its solemn treaties large numbers of homeless people were induced to move on to these lands and make settlements thereon, by a number of adventurers, chief among whom was one D. L. Payne.[8]

During one session of the International council it was reported that this man had succeeded in locating on these lands a large number of these settlers who were proceeding to make

[7]Created in 1867 with the tribe's removal from Kansas, the 480,000-acre Sac and Fox reservation was immediately west of the Creek domain and extended south from the Cimarron River to the North Canadian. Moses Keokuk, the son of Black Hawk's rival, stood for compromise and accommodation. The husband of two wives, in 1876 he and wife number two became Baptists, whereupon the latter left the marriage relationship, to the great chagrin of Keokuk. William T. Hagan, *The Sac and Fox Indians,* 233 and 251.

[8]Grayson refers here to the Boomer movement and its foremost leader, David L. Payne. Born in Indiana on Dec. 30, 1836, Payne came to Kansas Territory at the age of 22, served in the Union Army, was elected to the Kansas legislature, and held minor political posts in Washington, D.C. In 1879 he assumed leadership of a so-called Boomer group gathering along the southern border of Kansas, who were dedicated to white settlement of the so-called Unassigned Indian Lands situated in what is now central Oklahoma. These lands had been ceded by the Creeks and Seminoles in 1866 for the specific purpose of the resettlement of other Indian groups, but by 1879 had not been so assigned. Arguing that the lands were public and thus open to homestead entry, Payne led 18 members of his Oklahoma Colony to what is now Oklahoma City in April, 1880. The following month federal troops ushered them back to the Kansas border. A second attempt was made in July with 21 men, but with similar results. On the latter occasion, however, Payne and five others were taken to Fort Smith for trial on charges of violation of the 1834 Indian Intercourse Act. The case was docketed for the following March, 1881, and Payne was released. Stan Hoig, *David L. Payne: the Oklahoma Boomer,* chaps. 6, 7, and 8.

selections of land and to begin the building of homes. That body appointed a commission composed of one member from each of the Five Civilized Tribes to visit the invaded territory, and after investigation to take such steps as were deemed necessary to stop further encroachments. For this duty were assigned Mess. D. W. C. Duncan of the Cherokee nation, Judge [James] Thompson of the Choctaw nation, myself of the Creek nation, Governor [Benjamin] Frank Overton of the Chickasaw nation and Thomas Cloud of the Seminole nation. These men, with the exception of the Choctaw member, went out to the disputed territory and found the people settled there as had been currently stated, and after taking the situation in as near as may be, proceeded to have the government to arrest the man Payne and arraign him before the United States court at Ft. Smith, Arkansas, where Mr. Duncan and I, and I think one other of the Indian representatives appeared against him.[9] The Prosecuting attorney for the district, and Duncan for the Indians, argued the case before Isaac C. Parker, U.S. District Judge presiding. Payne was convicted and his presence forbidden in the Indian country. Having acted in this as representative of the Creek nation, I have deemed it proper to mention it in this connection.[10]

[9]Although the International Council had in March, 1880, appealed to the federal government to prevent the Boomer invasion of Indian Territory, it was an emergency October meeting of the Five Tribes that voted to send a delegation to Payne's camp. Grayson and his colleagues visited the Boomers near Caldwell, Kansas, on Dec. 17, 1880, just after they had aborted a third attempt to enter Oklahoma. He later wrote that they "observed about seventy five hungry, half-clad, back-woods white men, than whom a more worthless horde can hardly be found in all the balance of christendom." Of course, it was the United States Army rather than the Indian delegates that precipitated Payne's arrest. See G. W. Grayson, Okmulgee, to National Council, Oct., 1881, #30780, Foreign Relations Records, Creek Nation Papers, Manuscript Division, Oklahoma Historical Society; and Hoig, *David L. Payne*, 101.

[10]Payne's case was tried on March 7, 1881, before Judge Isaac Parker. Appointed in 1875 as federal judge for the Western District of Arkansas, Parker gained a reputation for harsh justice toward lawbreakers during a tenure on the bench that lasted until his death in Nov., 1896. U.S. District Attorney William H. H. Clayton prosecuted the case, ably assisted by Grayson and Duncan. Parker ruled on May 2, 1881, that title to the "Oklahoma lands" was still vested in the Creeks and Seminoles and thus Payne was an intruder. Because he was a two-time transgressor of the Intercourse Act, the Boomer was fined $1,000. See Carl Coke

It will be remembered that it is elsewhere stated that I was for several terms member of the national council. During that time and even when I was not a member, the chief and council deemed it advisable to include me with its representatives who were from time to time delegated to represent the interests of the nation at Washington. These were called delegates, and their duties varied at different times as the necessities of public interest seemed to dictate. There was no law or regulation by which any particular number of men had to be selected for this purpose, and sometimes as many as five were sent, not because so many men were needed to perform the duties in hand, nor yet because of their special qualification, but for the satisfaction of the full blood Indian element in the council, always largely in the majority, the ambitions of a few mixed bloods of strong influence, and the demand and necessity for some one actually competent and necessary to do the business with which the delegation was charged. The accommodation of these several factions always compelled the appointment of a large delegation, at a heavy expense, many of whom did, when so appointed, little other at Washington than to have a good time. These each were paid the same per diem at $7.00, traveling expenses of $200.00, with a smaller sum for common use in meeting incidental expenses.

We, the Creeks, have from first to last lost three such delegates at Washington. The first was an educated Indian of the Coweta town, a man of more than ordinary ability, named Daniel Asbury.[11] The next was also of the Coweta town, a full

Rister, " 'Oklahoma,' The Land of Promise, Part II," *Chronicles of Oklahoma* 23 (Spring, 1945): 7.

A Dartmouth College graduate in 1861, DeWitt Clinton Duncan was a noted Cherokee educator, writer, and attorney. See Kathleen Garrett, "Dartmouth Alumni in the Indian Territory," *Chronicles of Oklahoma* 32 (Summer, 1954): 123–41; and Dewitt Clinton Duncan, "Open Letter from Too-Qua-Stee to Congressman Charles Curtis, 1898," *Chronicles of Oklahoma* 47 (Autumn, 1969), 298–311.

[11] Grayson may be here referring to Daniel Aspberry, a Creek métis who was a successful merchant and, before the Civil War, a slave trader, who on at least two different occasions laid claim to Seminole slaves, took them, and then sold them. Upon what delegation he served is unknown. See Littlefield, *Africans and Creeks,* chap. 9.

blood Indian named Coweta Micco. I was with him when he died in a little second class hotel in Washington called the Tremont hotel.[12] The third was a full blood Indian of the Ah-beh-ka town named If-a Ema-thla. The first died in Washington from the effects of drink as I have been told. The nature of the illness of the second, although I was with him several times during his illness, I never learned. The third as I am informed died of an attack of pneumonia.

Up to the present time I have served as one of the principal business members of, as near as I can recall, seventeen of these Creek national delegations. My services as such have not been continuous during all that time, as some years passed when delegations were sent to Washington without me being numbered with them. I have always been proud of the fact that I was never elected a member of any delegation of which I was member through any persistent electioneering on my part as was done by others who succeeded in securing their election. I seemed to be put on these delegations because of my supposed education and general fitness for the work that had been committed to the delegation. In this connection I have to say that I have always regarded my own membership on these delegations as the highest honor that the nation could confer on me, as my appointment was not made to gratify the leaders of any faction, but seemingly from the confident belief in my individual trustworthiness and ability to properly represent the interests of the nation at so intelligent a government as that at Washington. I seemed always to have been put on these delegations for service that I was supposed to be competent to do and not for the mere accommodation either of myself or anyone else.

When the contest for the supremacy in the government between the constitutional party and those opposed became so serious that a respectable number of our people, under the leadership of Is-pa-heh-tsa, seceded and withdrew from the

---

[12]Coweta Micco, a Loyalist in the Civil War, helped write the Creek constitution of 1867, was a noted jurist and Methodist minister, opposed the Green Peach Rebellion, and was elected second chief in 1883. He died as a member of the 1885 delegation. Debo, *Road to Disappearance*, 171, 180, 228, 279, 282–83.

country and settled in the Comanche country, the Creek council delegated me and a full blood Indian named Jimmie Larney to proceed to Washington and if possible induce the government to send a military force to our country to teach these malcontented Creeks the necessity for obedience of the recognized laws of the nation.[13] My son, Walter, was then only a very small boy, but I took him with me, and with Robert Lincoln who was Secretary of War at that time and who was a stickler for the conventionalities of the ways of official business in Washington commonly called *red tape,* we experienced an annoying delay that kept us in that city much longer than we anticipated.[14] We succeeded, however, in causing the

[13] More often than not Is-pa-heh-tsa is spelled Isparhecher. A full-blood Creek born in 1829, Isparhecher was identified with the Lower Towns and the McIntosh faction of the tribe. He joined the First Creek Regiment of the Confederate Army, but during the 12 months of his enlistment was generally absent from duty. Like Sanford Perryman, he too mustered into the Union Army in 1863 at Fort Gibson, serving until his discharge in 1865. Although a devout Methodist and a holder of different offices under the Creek constitution of 1867, he emerged as a leader of that faction of the tribe—composed primarily of full bloods and freedmen—that supported that claims of Loyal Creeks and opposed a formal constitutional government.

A dispute between Creek freedmen and Cherokee cattlemen, a cession of land to the Seminoles, and an attempt to try Isparhecher for incest led in July, 1882, to an open conflict, known as the Green Peach War, between Isparhecher's followers and the supporters of Chief Samuel Checote. The tribal militia dispersed the insurgents east into the Cherokee Nation and west among the Seminoles, but in Dec., 1882, Isparhecher's adherents returned and fought a victorious battle 20 miles southwest of Okmulgee. The arrival of 50 federal soldiers at the capitol produced a brief calm. Reconciliation efforts failed, however, and in Feb., 1883, Pleasant Porter and an army of 700 Creek men pursued Isparhecher's forces into the Sac and Fox reservation, where the agent ordered Porter to withdraw. The insurgents then took refuge on the Washita River just east of the Wichita Indian Agency.

Grayson's fellow delegate at the time of the Green Peach War was not James Larney but Legus C. Perryman, later chief of the Creeks. Larney was the captain of the lighthorse defeated by Isparhecher's followers in Dec., 1882. In June, 1883, he did join Grayson on a delegation sent to Fort Gibson to protest subsistence of the insurgents at the expense of the Creek Nation. See Debo, *Road to Disappearance,* 271–79, and Samuel Checote, Muskogee Nation, to G. W. Grayson and L. C. Perryman, Feb. 2, 1883, File V-16, Box G-22, and Checote, Muskogee Nation, to Grayson and James Larney, June 15, 1883, Grayson Family Papers, Western History Collections, University of Oklahoma.

[14] Robert Todd Lincoln was the eldest and only surviving child of President and Mrs. Abraham Lincoln. He served as secretary of war between 1881 and 1885. Dumas Malone, ed., *Dictionary of American Biography* 11:267.

Isparhecher, leader of the Green Peach Rebellion and principal chief of the
Creeks from 1895 to 1899. *Oklahoma Historical Society.*

War Department to send a detachment of soldiers under command of a commissioned officer to our country and after
Is-pa-heh-tsa and his followers, rounding up and bringing
them back to the Creek nation and through the nation to Fort
Gibson in the Cherokee nation.[15]

In my earlier delegateships to Washington our work consisted principally in opposition to the influence of railroad cor-
porations who were all the while working to induce the government to violate its treaty stipulations with our nation and

[15]Federal troops from Fort Gibson and Fort Sill under the command of Maj.
J. C. Bates located Isparhecher's encampment on April 23, 1883. After a suggestion of resistance, the insurgents broke and ran but were later gathered up and
returned to Fort Gibson, where they remained until passions cooled. In August
at a conference attended by Grayson, the two factions compromised their differences, but without major modifications of the existing constitutional government.
Debo, *Road to Disappearance,* 278–80.

extend a territorial form of government over our nation and territory, the advantages to the railroads being that such a change would soon precipitate statehood and with it increased business for the roads. Many scores of bills from first to last were introduced into Congress proposing a territorial form of government for the Indian territory, against which such proposals the Five Civilized Tribes were a unit. The delegates from these tribes were usually specifically instructed to oppose all such measures, and indeed were for a long time successful.[16]

On one occasion the politics of our nation, which for a number of years involved the issue as to whether the intelligence residing principally in the people who had espoused the contentions of the Confederacy in the late war should shape and conduct the government of the nation—with the balances always oscillating in favor of the southerners—became somewhat mixed. Men who had been irretrievably divided by the questions and facts of the late war, for the purposes of political success, made strange compromises on matters of policy and on the question of filling important offices in our government. A general election was held throughout the nation for principal chief and other officers, in which the voters who had been South and those who had been North were to be found in all kinds of alignment and the vote was a very close one.

As well as I can now recall, there were three candidates running for the chieftaincy, namely J. M. Perryman, Samuel Checote and Is-pa-heh-tsa.[17] Checote, who had been our chief during the war and even many years afterwards, had now lost his hold on the favor of the people, and his supporters in the election polled so few votes that he was very little considered in the canvass of the votes cast. But while this was so, he still wielded some influence and weight in our national affairs. The race for the office then was between J. M. Perryman, one of our best men who had stood in the ranks of the soldiers of the

[16] For an excellent study of the interrelatedness of the railroad and territorial bills, see H. Craig Miner, *The Corporation and the Indian: Tribal Sovereignty and Industrial Civilization in Indian Territory, 1865–1907.*

[17] Grayson refers here to the election of 1883, the campaign for which began immediately after the settlement of the Green Peach War. See Chap. 8, n. 8; Chap. 9, n. 9; and n. 13 in this chapter.

South and who had always until now been a supporter of Checote, and Is-pa-heh-tsa, an adherent of the cause of the north. After the counting of the votes it was ascertained that Perryman had won out by a small plurality of, if I mistake not, thirty three.[18] Is-pa-heh-tsa, aided by the negroes and a few others, in a rather high-handed manner declared and claimed that he had been elected chief and was the only one entitled to the office. Checote threw what influence he had left to the support of Is-pa-heh-tsa, and the nation and our council were left in an anomalous condition.[19]

The council, however, previous to this anomaly had provided a delegation to look after its affairs in Washington, which delegation had been nominated by Checote and confirmed by the old and retiring council. This delegation consisted of Is-pa-heh-tsa, Checote, David M. Hodge and myself. S. B. Callahan was with Checote and Is-pa, but I think his rank was that of Clerk only.[20] Our council instructed me and

[18] After the council had thrown out disputed votes from three towns, Perryman received 641 votes; Checote, 608; and Isparhecher, 486. None won the majority required by the English version of the constitution, but the words "plurality" and "majority" had the same meaning in Creek. Perryman took the oath of office on Dec. 5, 1883. Debo, *Road to Disappearance*, 281–83.

[19] A new council convened with newly elected membership favorable to Isparhecher the day after the adjournment of the old body that had invalidated the disputed returns. This council recounted the votes, admitted the ballots from the three towns, and declared Isparhecher elected chief by a vote of 682 to 645 for Perryman and 611 for Checote. On Dec. 18, Isparhecher took the oath of office. Debo, *Road to Disappearance*, 283.

[20] The delegation proceeded to Washington in Jan., 1884. Maternally related to the Perrymans and the first cousin of A. P. McKellop, David M. Hodge was born at Choska in 1841. During the Civil War he identified with the Loyal Creeks and fought in the Union Army. Well educated at Presbyterian mission schools and coauthor of a Creek dictionary and grammar, he helped write the constitution of 1867, frequently served as clerk of the national council, and was a frequent member of delegations to Washington. Hodge was one of the Creeks that negotiated the original allotment embodied in the Curtis Act of 1898. Samuel Benton Callahan, a white man with little Creek blood, became a member of the tribe in 1858. He represented the Creeks in the Confederate States Congress, was a close friend of Isparhecher, and served as secretary to Perryman. Ironically, Callahan wrote the acceptance speeches used by both of the two disputing candidates for the chieftaincy in Dec., 1883. See Debo, *Road to Disappearance*, 158, 177, 180, 273, 283, and 308; Carolyn Thomas Foreman, "The Yuchi: Children of the Sun," *Chronicles of Oklahoma* 37 (Winter, 1959–60): 480–96; and Muriel H.

Creek delegation to Washington, D.C., 1908. From left to right, standing, Samuel J. Haynes and Johnson Tiger; seated, H. L. Mott (tribal attorney), Moty Tiger (chief), and G. W. Grayson. *Smithsonian Institution, Bureau of American Ethnology.*

Hodge to take up the question of the chieftaincy of the Creek nation with the Secretary of the Interior, who at that time was Henry M. Teller of Colorado. Here was certainly a house divided against itself: the late chief Checote, and the candidate whom he declared was elected in the late election, and two other delegates with instructions to oppose their contentions.[21]

I was in this contest placed in a very embarrassing position, being called upon by my council to oppose the contention of a former old chief with the aid of Hodge, who was of no earthly use to me, being as he appeared to be a friend of the cause of

Wright, "Appendix: Samuel Benton Callahan," *Chronicles of Oklahoma* 35 (Autumn, 1955): 314–15.339

[21] United States senator from Colorado both before and after his service as secretary of the interior, Henry M. Teller held the administrative post between April, 1882, and March, 1885. Teller was unusual among federal officials in that he opposed allotment of Indian lands. *Biographical Directory of the American Congresses, 1774–1961,* 1697.

the other side when in their company and in sympathy with our position when with me. We had several conferences with the Secretary and his assistant general and the question dragged for many weeks. I remember becoming fearful lest the other side succeed in impressing the Interior department with the idea that J. M. Perryman, the man I was contending had been legally elected chief, was a highly educated man having much the appearance of a white man, and fifty years ahead of the people over whom he was claiming to have been elected chief. [As this] view might prejudice his case in the eyes of the Secretary, I wired Perryman to come at once, after asking Secretary Teller to hold up action for a few days.

Perryman was very dark complexioned, quite as much so as a full blood Indian, and a man of limited education but of great good common sense, and I knew his presence would disabuse the Secretary's mind of any prejudice he may have conceived against him, if any. He came on, and after paying the Secretary a call of respect, I informed that dignitary that I would be pleased if he would decide our case at as early a day as possible. In a short time afterward he called before him all who were interested in the final decision and without any extended talk explaining how he came to the conclusion, he announced that his decision was that J. M. Perryman had been legally elected chief and that he would be recognized by the government as the lawful chief of the nation. The defeated candidate, Is-pa-heh-tsa and entourage, he advised to counsel their following not to continue any wrangling over the election as it was now finally decided, but to obey the recognized government and laws of the nation. Although David M. Hodge was associated with me with equal authority to present and insist on the views of our government in this contest, he did so little toward promoting the end attained that I have not deemed it usurious or unjust when I claim quite all the credit for this victory.[22]

I occupied a position in this contest that was characterized

[22] Teller made his decision on Feb. 27, 1884. Isparhecher was a candidate for principal chief in 1887, 1891, and again in 1895. He won the post in the latter election, serving until 1899. He died in 1902. See H. M. Teller, Washington, to

by a feature that was repugnant to me and to a well grounded policy of the Creek and other civilized nations of the Indian territory at that time. These nations were very jealous of their rights of self-government which had been solemnly recognized and even guaranteed by the terms of treaties with the government then in force. That would include the settlement of just such questions as that now before us; but for us to waive that right and ask the government to interfere and effect a settlement between us in a purely local question had the appearance of discovering incompetence for self-government on our part, besides creating a circumstance which might in the future be taken advantage of as a precedent that gave license for the United States to interfere in other of our national questions and render decisions whether agreeable or not, thus in effect abrogating our cherished right of self-government.

My missions to Washington after this had for their objects sometimes the inducement of the government to make *per capita* payments to our people of large sums of the national funds, but the most of my work has been that of begging Congress not to violate the terms of its treaties and agreements with our people and pass a territorial form of government over them in the manner being demanded and urged by representatives of the surrounding states. The united [opposition] efforts of the Indian delegations of the Five Civilized Tribes of the Indian territory may be said to have been successful, as such forms of government was never extended over the Indians, although it was continually urged with unceasing diligence by members of Congress from adjoining states.

Instead of extending over us a territorial form of government, the Congress of the United States passed a law creating what was called the Dawes Commission, which was so designated because the senator from Massachusetts Henry L. Dawes originated the bill and was placed at the head of the commission when it was appointed under the law. [The commission] was given authority to meet and confer with the au-

---

Commissioner of Indian Affairs, Feb. 27, 1884, File VI-8, Box G-23, Grayson Family Papers, Western History Collections, University of Oklahoma.

Creek Indians en route to vote, circa 1903. *Western History Collections, University of Oklahoma Library.*

thorities of the Five Tribes and negotiate for the abolishment of their several tribal governments, the sectionization of their lands, and individualization of the same.[23]

Here was a proposal which paralyzed the Indians for a time with its bold effrontery. Here we, a people who had been a self-governing people for hundreds and possibly a thousand

[23] Not to be confused with the 1887 Dawes Act, which exempted the Five Civilized Tribes from its provisions, Congress created and empowered the so-

years, who had a government and administered its affairs ages before such an entity as the United States was ever dreamed of, are asked and admonished that we must give up all idea of local government, change our system of land holding to that which we confidently believed had pauperized thousands of white people—all for why; not because we had violated any treaties with the United States which guaranteed in solemn terms our undisturbed possession of these; not because of any respectable number of intelligent Indians were clamoring for a change of conditions; not because any non-enforcement of law prevailed to a greater extent in the Indian territory than elsewhere; but simply because regardless of the plain dictates of justice and a christian conscience, the ruthless restless white man demanded it. Demanded it because in the general upheaval that would follow the change he, the white man, hoped and expected to obtain for a song, lands from ignorant Indians as others had done in other older states.

---

called Dawes Commission in March, 1893, to negotiate with representatives of the Five Tribes for the allotment in severalty of their domains. The Creeks and the other of the Five Civilized tribes refused to discuss the topic, whereupon Congress in 1895 and 1896 authorized the commission to survey tribal lands and enroll allottees without tribal assent. And in 1898 the Curtis Act directed that allotment begin with or without Creek consent. In the meantime federal officials marked 3,079,000 acres and counted 18,761 Creeks, 6,809 of whom were freedmen. In March, 1900, tribal leaders finally accepted an allotment agreement by which every man, woman, and child (red and black) received individual title to 160 acres and by which tribal government was dissolved on or before March 4, 1906. See Angie Debo, *And Still the Waters Run,* 33, 47, 51.

Bibliography

Manuscript Sources

Western History Collections, University of Oklahoma, Norman, Oklahoma
  Grayson Family Papers
Manuscript Division, Oklahoma Historical Society, Oklahoma City, Oklahoma
  Creek Nation Papers: Election Records, Foreign Relation Records, Misc. Section X, National Council Records, Pasture Records, Treasurer Records.
  Grant Foreman Collection: Thomas Meagher Maps.
  Kiowa Tribal Papers: Foreign Relations Records.
  Records of the Dawes Commission: Creek Allotment Rolls.

Government Documents

Acts and Resolutions of the National Council of the Muskogee Nation of 1893 and 1899, inclusive. Reprint. Washington, D.C.: Scholarly Resources, Inc., 1975.
Annual Report of the Commissioner of Indian Affairs. 1841–59.
Biographical Directory of the American Congress, 1774–1961. Washington, D.C.: Government Printing Office, 1961.
The War of Rebellion: A Compilation of the Official Records of the Union and Confederate Armies. Series i, vol. 22, pt. 1; vol. 34, pt. 1; vol. 41, pt. 1. Washington, D.C.: Government Printing Office, 1888–98.

Newspapers

(Atoka) *The Vindicator,* July 3, 1875
(Eufaula) *Indian Journal,* Dec. 2 and 9, 1920
(Fort Gibson) *Indian Arrow,* July 25, 1889
Muskogee Phoenix, July 25, 1889
(Oklahoma City) *The Daily Oklahoman,* July 14, 1920
Tulsa Tribune, Dec. 3, 1920

Books

Baxter, William. *Pea Ridge and Prairie Grove.* Cincinnati: Poe and Hitchcock, 1864.
Benedict, John D. *Muskogee and Northeastern Oklahoma.* 4 vols. Chicago: S. J. Clarke Publishing Co., 1922.
Britton, Wiley. *The Union Indian Brigade in the Civil War.* Kansas City: Franklin Hudson Publishing Co., 1922.
Campbell's Abstract of Creek Indian Census Cards and Index. Muskogee: Phoenix Job Printing Company, 1915.
Caughey, John W. *McGillivray of the Creeks.* Norman: University of Oklahoma Press, 1939.
Collections of the Georgia Historical Society. Vol. 3. Savannah: Georgia Historical Society, 1848.
Cunningham, Frank. *General Stand Watie's Confederate Indians.* San Antonio: Naylor Company, 1959.
Debo, Angie. *The Road to Disappearance: A History of the Creek Indians.* Norman: University of Oklahoma Press, 1979.
———. *And Still the Waters Run: The Betrayal of the Five Civilized Tribes.* Princeton, N.J.: Princeton University Press, 1972. Reprint, Norman: University of Oklahoma Press, 1984.
Eckstein, Stephen Daniel, Jr. *History of the Churches of Christ in Texas, 1824–1950.* Austin: Firm Foundation Publishing House, 1963.
Eggleston, George Cary. *Red Eagle and the Wars with the Creek Indians of Alabama.* New York: Dodd, Mead Co., 1878.

Fischer, LeRoy H., ed. *The Civil War Era in Indian Territory.* Los Angeles: Lorrin L. Morrison, Publisher, 1974.

Foreman, Carolyn T. *Park Hill.* Muskogee: Star Printery, 1948.

Foreman, Grant. *Lore and Lure of Eastern Oklahoma.* Muskogee: Muskogee Chamber of Commerce, n.d.

————. *Indian Removal.* Norman: University of Oklahoma Press, 1932.

————. *The Five Civilized Tribes.* Norman: University of Oklahoma Press, 1934.

————. *Down the Texas Road.* Norman: University of Oklahoma Press, 1936.

Franks, Kenny A. *Stand Watie and the Agony of the Cherokee Nation.* Memphis: Memphis State University Press, 1979.

Gibson, A. M. *The Kickapoos: Lords of the Middle Border.* Norman: University of Oklahoma Press, 1963.

————. *Oklahoma: A History of Five Centuries.* 2d ed. Norman: University of Oklahoma Press, 1981.

Gideon, D. C. *Indian Territory.* New York: Lewis Publishing Company, 1901.

Green, Donald E. *The Creek People.* Phoenix: Indian Tribal Series, 1973.

Green, Michael D. *The Politics of Indian Removal: Creek Government and Society in Crisis.* Lincoln: University of Nebraska Press, 1982.

Hagan, William T. *The Sac and Fox Indians.* Norman: University of Oklahoma Press, 1958.

————. *United States–Comanche Relations: The Reservation Years.* New Haven: Yale University Press, 1976.

Hastain's Township Plats of the Creek Nation. Muskogee: n.p., n.d.

Hawkins, Benjamin. *A Sketch of the Creek Country.* New York: Kraus Reprint Co., 1971.

Henri, Florette. *Benjamin Hawkins and the Southern Indians.* Norman: University of Oklahoma Press, 1986.

History of Benton, Washington, Carroll, Madison, Crawford, Franklin and Sebastian Counties, Arkansas. Chicago: Goodspeed Publishing Co., 1889.

Hoig, Stan. *David L. Payne: the Oklahoma Boomer.* Oklahoma City: Western Heritage Books, 1980.

Hudson, Charles. *The Southern Indians.* Knoxville: University of Tennessee Press, 1976.

Littlefield, Daniel F., Jr. *Africans and Creeks, From the Colonial Period to the Civil War.* Westport, Conn.: Greenwood Press, 1979.

Malone, Dumas, ed. *Dictionary of American Biography.* 23 vols. New York: Charles Scribner's Sons, 1933.

Maxwell, Amos D. *The Sequoyah Constitutional Convention.* Boston: Meador Publishing Co., c. 1953.

Miner, H. Craig. *The Corporation and the Indian: Tribal Sovereignty and Industrial Civilization in Indian Territory, 1865–1907.* Columbia: University of Missouri Press, 1976.

Morris, John W., Charles R. Goins, and Edwin C. McReynolds. *Historical Atlas of Oklahoma.* 2d ed. Norman: University of Oklahoma Press, 1976.

Moulton, Gary E. *John Ross: Cherokee Chief.* Athens: University of Georgia Press, 1978.

O'Beirne, H. F., and E. S. O'Beirne. *The Indian Territory: Its Chiefs, Legislators, and Leading Men.* Vol. 1. St. Louis: C. B. Woodward Company, 1892.

Owsley, Frank Lawrence, Jr. *Struggle for the Gulf Borderlands: The Creek Wars and the Battle of New Orleans, 1812–1813.* Gainesville: University Presses of Florida, 1981.

Pickett, Andrew J. *History of Alabama and Incidentally, of Georgia and Mississippi from the Earliest Period.* Birmingham: Webb Book Company, 1900.

Rampp, Larry C., and Donald L. Rampp. *The Civil War in the Indian Territory.* Austin: Presidial Press, 1975.

Remini, Robert V. *Andrew Jackson and the Course of American Empire, 1767–1821.* New York: Harper and Row, 1977.

Ruth, Kent, et al. *Oklahoma: A Guide to the Sooner State.* Rev. ed. Norman: University of Oklahoma Press, c. 1957.

———. *Oklahoma Travel Handbook.* Norman: University of Oklahoma Press, 1977.

Wardell, Morris L. *A Political History of the Cherokee Nation, 1838–1907.* Norman: University of Oklahoma Press, 1938.

Wright, Muriel H. *A Guide to the Indian Tribes of Oklahoma.* Norman: University of Oklahoma Press, 1951.

———— and LeRoy H. Fischer. *Civil War Sites in Oklahoma.* Oklahoma City: Oklahoma Historical Society, 1967.

Articles

Applen, Allen G. "An Attempted Indian State Government: The Okmulgee Constitution in Indian Territory, 1870–1876." *Kansas Quarterly* 3 (Fall, 1971): 89–99.

Debo, Angie. "Southern Refugees of the Cherokee Nation." *Southwestern Historical Quarterly* 35 (April, 1932): 255–66.

Donat, Pat. "Arkansas College: The Beginning." *Flashback,* Aug., 1977, 1–6.

Duncan, Dewitt Clinton. "Open letter from Too-Qua-Stee to Congressman Charles Curtis, 1898." *Chronicles of Oklahoma* 47 (Autumn, 1969): 298–304.

East, Mary L. " 'Mr. Graham's School,' State's First College." (Little Rock) *Arkansas Gazette,* Oct. 21, 1945, 1 and 23.

Foreman, Carolyn Thomas. "The Coody Family of Indian Territory." *Chronicles of Oklahoma* 25 (Winter, 1947): 323–41.

———. "North Fork Town." *Chronicles of Oklahoma* 29 (Spring, 1951): 79–111.

———. "S. Alice Callahan: Author of Wynema child of the Forest." *Chronicles of Oklahoma* 33 (Autumn, 1955): 305–15.

———. "The Light-Horsemen of Indian Territory." *Chronicles of Oklahoma* 34 (Spring, 1956): 17–43.

———. "Two Notable Women of the Creek Nation." *Chronicles of Oklahoma* 35 (Autumn, 1957): 315–37.

———. "The Yuchi: Children of the Sun." *Chronicles of Oklahoma* 37 (Winter, 1959–60): 480–96.

———. "Notes on Dewitt Clinton Duncan and a Recently Discovered History of the Cherokee." *Chronicles of Oklahoma* 47 (Autumn, 1969): 305–11.

Foreman, Grant. "The California Overland Trail Route Through

Oklahoma." *Chronicles of Oklahoma* 9 (Sept., 1931): 300–317.

―――. "Early Post Offices of Oklahoma." *Chronicles of Oklahoma* 6 (March, 1928): 4–25.

Garrett, Kathleen. "Dartmouth Alumni in the Indian Territory." *Chronicles of Oklahoma* 32 (Summer, 1954): 123–41.

"Grierson, Sir Robert." *Dictionary of National Biography* 8:664–65. Reprint, London: Oxford University Press, 1949–50.

Hancock, Marvin J. "The Second Battle of Cabin Creek, 1864." *Chronicles of Oklahoma* 34 (Winter, 1961–62): 414–26.

"Journal of the Adjourned Session of First General Council of the Indian Territory." *Chronicles of Oklahoma* 3 (April, 1925): 33–44.

Lee, Keun Sang. "The Capture of the *J. R. Williams.*" *Chronicles of Oklahoma* 55 (Spring, 1982): 22–38.

Meserve, John Bartlett. "Chief Pleasant Porter." *Chronicles of Oklahoma* 9 (Sept., 1931): 318–34.

―――. "The MacIntoshes." *Chronicles of Oklahoma* 10 (Sept., 1932): 310–25.

―――. "The Perrymans." *Chronicles of Oklahoma* 15 (June, 1937): 166–85.

―――. "Chief Lewis Downing and Chief Charles Thompson." *Chronicles of Oklahoma* 16 (Sept., 1983): 315–25.

―――. "Chief Samuel Checote, with Sketches of Chiefs Locher Harjo and Ward Coachman." *Chronicles of Oklahoma* 16 (Dec., 1938): 401–409.

Morton, Ohland. "The Government of the Creek Nation, Part I." *Chronicles of Oklahoma* 8 (March, 1930): 42–64.

―――. "The Government of the Creek Nation, Part II." *Chronicles of Oklahoma* 8 (June, 1930): 190–225.

―――. "Reconstruction in the Creek Nation." *Chronicles of Oklahoma* 9 (June, 1931): 171–79.

"Notes and Documents." *Chronicles of Oklahoma* 44 (Aug., 1966): 322–24.

Rister, Carl Coke. " 'Oklahoma,' The Land of Promise, Part II." *Chronicles of Oklahoma* 23 (Spring, 1945): 2–7.

Routh, E. C. "Henry Friedland Buckner." *Chronicles of Oklahoma* 14 (Dec., 1936): 456–66.

Swanton, John R. "Religious Beliefs and Medical Practices of the Creek Indians." In *Forty-second Annual Report of the Bureau of American Ethnology*, pp. 437–672. Washington, D.C.: Government Printing Office, 1928.

———. "Social Organization and Social Usages of the Indians of the Creek Confederacy." In *Forty-second Annual Report of the Bureau of American Ethnology*, pp. 23–436.

Wilson, L. M. S. "Reminiscenses of Jim Tomm." *Chronicles of Oklahoma* 44 (Autumn, 1966): 290–306.

Wilson, T. Paul. "Delegates of the Five Civilized Tribes in the Confederate Congress." *Chronicles of Oklahoma* 53 (Fall, 1975): 353–66.

Wright, Muriel H. "Wapanucka Academy, Chickasaw Nation." *Chronicles of Oklahoma* 12 (Dec., 1934): 402–31.

———. "General Douglas H. Cooper, C.S.A.." *Chronicles of Oklahoma* 32 (Summer, 1954): 142–84.

———. "Appendix: Samuel Benton Callahan." *Chronicles of Oklahoma* 33 (Autumn, 1955): 314–15.

———. "A Report to the General Council at Okmulgee in 1873." *Chronicles of Oklahoma* 34 (Spring, 1956): 8–16.

———. "The Butterfield Overland Mail One Hundred Years Ago." *Chronicles of Oklahoma* 35 (Spring, 1957): 55–71.

Theses and Dissertations

Lanford, Annelle Sharp. "North Fork to Eufaula, 1836–1907." M.A. thesis, University of Oklahoma, 1954.

Moffitt, James William. "A History of Early Baptist Missions Among the Five Civilized Tribes." Ph.D. diss., University of Oklahoma, 1946.

Index